**ROUGH
GUIDES**

POCKET **ROUGH GUIDE**
MALTA & GOZO

this third edition updated by
DANIEL STABLES

CONTENTS

MALTA

Has any other tiny archipelago contributed so much to the history books? What sets Malta apart from other island destinations is the sheer number of historic sites, cultural attractions and ancient monuments squeezed onto its 246 square kilometres. With a dizzying number of World Heritage Sights for its size – inescapable reminders of its complicated 7000-year-old-history – Malta feels like a huge open-air museum. But that doesn't mean it's stuck in the past; in recent years Malta has truly come into its own as an alluring, quirky and rewarding destination. An abundance of top-notch restaurants, charming villages, brightly painted balconies, bustling promenades, vintage cars and warm hospitality means this little island leaves a big impression.

The intricately decorated interior of St John's Co-Cathedral

The majority of Malta's historical sights are concentrated in Valletta and the "Three Cities", laid out around the Grand Harbour and marked by immense limestone walls. These impressive fortifications are a legacy of its complex history; Malta has alternated between long spells of isolation and brief outbursts of momentousness during periods of conflict when the island's strategic location at the centre of the Mediterranean gave it a significance disproportionate to its size. There are plenty of opportunities to get to grips with Malta's military past, with a host of impenetrable forts and several museums dedicated to the islands' crucial role during World War II and the Great Siege of 1565, when the Order of the Knights of St John repelled a six-month attack by invading Turks. The Grand Harbour's fortifications enclose a host of extravagant churches and palaces, the legacy of the Knights, who ruled the island for the next three hundred years. While the Baroque designs of the Knights are ever-present, the Neolithic era made an equally significant mark

Statue of Queen Victoria, Valletta

on the islands. The magnificent outdoor and underground temples across Malta and Gozo are the oldest freestanding man-made structures in the world, pre-dating Egypt's pyramids. Second to none, there are more major Neolithic complexes here than in the whole of the rest of Europe.

When to visit

The most popular time to visit is in high season (May–Oct). In July and August, when the Maltese also take their summer holidays, the island can feel suffocatingly hot and crowded, but it's a lively time to visit, coinciding with plenty of festivals and annual village feasts. Rain is nearly unheard of between May and September, and the countryside is parched and dry. Scorching temperatures make sightseeing difficult during the middle of the day, but evenings bring relief and life to village squares and promenades well into the night. Things get quieter in the low season (Oct–May), when the weather is mild, rain comes in intense but infrequent bursts, and the countryside is vividly green (though mosquitoes can be bothersome). The sea is too cold for swimming, but comfortable temperatures make sightseeing very pleasant. Outside of the high season, the best times to visit are the autumn or spring shoulder seasons. Festivals continue into the autumn and the sea remains balmy, while in the spring, the countryside is ablaze with wildflowers.

Terrone

A short boat-ride from Malta, Gozo has a more rural character than its sister island. What it lacks in the number of historic attractions of the mainland, it makes up for with tranquility, natural beauty and an amenable Mediterranean lifestyle. Hilly topography, ravishing coastal cliffs and striking salt pans offer marvellous walks, while the dive sites offshore are widely acknowledged as some of the best in the Mediterranean.

Though a small island, it can take a while to travel on Malta's congested roads, even by bus (there are six cars for every ten people on the archipelago). Malta's public-transport system is modern and robust, servicing the entire country, including the sparsely populated countryside. Buses typically run from 5am to 11pm, sometimes at night, and you pay for a 2-hour pass. More economical and convenient is the Explore Card, which offers one week of unlimited public bus travel and two ferry trips between Valletta, Sliema

and the Three Cities. Travelling by foot or ferry can often be a faster option, particularly around Sliema, St Julian's and Valletta (be sure to make eye contact with drivers before crossing the road). Double-decker private hop-on hop-off bus tours are also convenient for touring Malta's major attractions (1-day pass). Renting a car will free independent travellers to stray off the beaten path, but is not for the faint of heart. Driving styles here are aggressive at best and chaotic at worst, with road rules inconsistently observed and road conditions quite poor in some areas. However, reasonable rental fees make this an economic option for families and groups. Renting a motorbike or scooter offers a faster way to bypass traffic on congested roads, but again, can be perilous. Cycling is just beginning to gain popularity in Malta and with very few bicycle lanes and a hilly topography, casual cyclists will find it nearly impossible to travel on two wheels (especially under the scorching summer sun).

Where to...

Shop

Undoubtedly, Malta's riches lie in its plethora of cultural attractions – not its shops – but there are a few gems to uncover amongst its monotonous selection of high-street outlets and souvenir shacks. For your pick of handmade treasures head to Gozo, where artisan lace, reed baskets, leather goods and local delicacies are readily found throughout Victoria and the Ta Dbieġi Crafts Village. On Malta, you'll find a Mdina Glass shop in every major village; a sure bet for gorgeous glass creations. For fashionistas, Sliema and Valletta are the places to see and be seen, with shopping malls and a few boutiques from local designers.
OUR FAVOURITES: Souvenirs That Don't Suck, see page 60. Ta Dbieġi Crafts Village, see page 119. Charles & Ron, see page 41.

Eat

Dining out is an essential part of Maltese social life; according to national statistics, Maltese families spend as much at restaurants as they do on rent and utilities. Malta is home to an astonishing number of restaurants: about 2300 at last count! Sliema, St Julian's and Valletta are brimming with mid-priced and upmarket restaurants, mostly Mediterranean, Italian and Asian. Further afield, local pizza, pasta and burger joints are reliable for cheap eats. A Maltese favourite is the huge, long and boozy Sunday lunch, served at almost every restaurant but particularly popular at sea or countryside outlets.
OUR FAVOURITES: Harbour Club, see page 43. Terrone, see page 103. Fernandō Gastrotheque, see page 62.

Drink

The ratio of bars to churches in Malta is easily three to one – impressive, given the island is home to more than 359 churches. Visit Valletta for atmospheric wine bars and elegant cocktail lounges (both often have live music), or Sliema for drinks with a view at its plentiful seaside kiosks. For a cheap pint in any village, the *kazin* (a marching-band club-cum-community centre) is a favourite of locals. The Italian aperitivo tradition is alive and well in Malta; most establishments see a rush of patrons from 6pm for aperitifs and small bites.
OUR FAVOURITES: Charles Grech, see page 44. Il-Gabbana, see page 61. Hole in the Wall, see page 63.

Go out

The village of Paċeville, enclosed by sprawling seaside resorts and a small beach, is the centre of Malta's nightlife scene. Techno and hip-hop clubs, British-style pubs and cocktail bars occupy most of its ten-block radius, making it a particularly popular destination for stag and hen dos. In the summer, the party scene shifts from Paċeville to the massive outdoor club complexes around Ta Qali National Park, and the seaside lidos in Buġibba and Sliema, which compete to host the most impressive parties every weekend.
OUR FAVOURITES: Havana Club, see page 62. Hugo's Terrace, see page 63. Café del Mar Lido, see page 86.

Malta and Gozo at a glance

Gozo p.104.
With quiet villages clustered around gigantic parish churches, and a population whose hospitality is legendary, Gozo offers a peaceful, pastoral alternative to Malta. Unplug and unwind here while discovering rustic Gozitan food and a slower pace of life.

The north p.80.
With numerous small sandy beaches and a sparsely populated hilly countryside, the north is ideal for sun-seeking sojourns and peaceful hikes.

Mdina and Rabat p.64.
Mdina was first settled by the Phoenicians, but is characterized by its marvellous Arab-period medieval architecture, Baroque palaces and limestone cathedral. Twisting alleys have kept vehicles and modernity at bay here. Admiring the expansive views of the entire island from atop the citadel's looming fortifications, it's easy to see the strategic importance of this ancient capital.

Central Malta p.74.
So densely populated it's impossible to tell where one village ends and another begins, central Malta offers few tourist attractions but an authentic slice of everyday life.

The south p.94.
Dramatic cliffs, colourfully quaint fishing villages and four Neolithic temples (the most stunning is the Hypogeum) make the south a must on any itinerary.

| 0 | miles | 2 |
| 0 | kilometres | 4 |

Comino p.122.
The tiny islet of Comino is home to the famously crystal clear turquoise waters of the Blue Lagoon, as well as some scenic coastal walks. The best time to visit is in the spring, when the rocky garigue habitat comes into bloom.

The Three Cities p.46.
Characterized by a medieval urban fabric of close-knit Baroque architecture, the "Three Cities" are home to Knightly palaces and forts handsomely contrasted by a more recently constructed superyacht marina.

Valletta p.26.
The churches, palaces, fortifications and grand public buildings of Malta's capital city – designated a World Heritage Site in its entirety – have remained largely unchanged since their construction more than 450 years ago. Charming architecture, modern museums, and Malta's best restaurants make Valletta an eclectic and essential place to explore.

Sliema and St Julian's p.54.
Once a sheltered fishing village, Sliema was the location of Malta's first holiday resort in the 1970s, with St Julian's not far behind. Today, this lively 5km stretch of coastline is home to an impressive array of cafés, bars and restaurants.

Mistra Bay
Salina Bay
Buġibba
St Paul's Bay

N

Paceville
Naxxar
St Julian's
Mosta
Sliema
Gzira
Malta
Balzan
VALLETTA
Attard
Ħamrun
Marsa
Paola
Ħaż Żebbuġ

Siġġiewi
Luqa
Tarxien
Marsascala
Żejtun
Mqabba
Marsaxlokk
Qrendi
Żurrieq
Birżebbuġa
Marsaxlokk Bay
St Peter's Pool
Xrobb L-Għaġin
Blue Grotto

15 Things not to miss

It's not possible to see everything that Malta has to offer in one trip – and we don't propose you try. What follows is a selective taste of the islands' highlights, from Baroque architecture to stunning coastal landscapes.

> Gozo's Citadel
See page 106
Offering panoramic views of much of Gozo, and home to no fewer than four museums, a cathedral and a superb interpretation centre, the compact, honey-coloured Citadel punches far above its weight.

< Valletta
See page 26
If you only visit one place in Malta it must be Valletta. This alluring Baroque capital is home to the country's major museums, besides stunning architecture, lush gardens, lavish churches, hip bars and restaurants, and remnants of a unique local culture.

∨ Ħaġar Qim and Mnajdra Temple Complex
See page 99
The beauty of these two spectacular Neolithic temples is enhanced by their location on a cliff head overlooking the sea and the untouched Maltese countryside.

< **Mdina**
See page 64
Visitors are swept back in time in the marvellous medieval city of Mdina, where charming winding alleys have kept modernity at bay.

∨ **Ħal Saflieni Hypogeum**
See page 95
The stirring and mysterious atmosphere of this stunningly preserved 3600 BCE underground temple complex – a UNESCO World Heritage Site older than Egypt's pyramids or Stonehenge – cannot be overstated.

∧ **Dwejra, Gozo**
See page 117
Though its most famous landmark – the Azure Window – was lost forever to a winter storm in 2017, Dwejra's Inland Sea and stunning coastal landscape remain must-sees on any Gozo itinerary.

< **The Marsaxlokk Fish Market**
See page 101
A chaotic, colourful feast for the senses, the market in this picturesque fishing village is a great place to see – and feast on – local seafood.

∧ Fort St Elmo & The National War Museum
See page 39
This superb museum – located in a beautifully restored sixteenth-century fort overlooking two harbours – traces the history of military activity in Malta from the Great Siege of 1565 to World War II.

∨ Sliema & St Julian's Promenade
See page 54
For a taste of local life, take a stroll (or a dip) along the pretty seaside promenade in cosmopolitan Sliema and St Julian's.

∧ **The Blue Grotto, Malta**
See page 100
A dramatic, naturally formed buttress shelters a huge domed cave known for its deep-blue luminous waters.

< **St John's Co-Cathedral**
See page 33
Commissioned by Grand Master Jean de la Cassière and designed by Girolamo Cassar, this opulent building is dedicated to the Order's patron saint, John the Baptist.

< **Malta at War Museum**
See page 47
The star attraction of this lovely little museum in Birgu is an underground labyrinth of rock-cut World War II shelters.

∨ **Għajn Tuffieħa beach**
See page 90
This large sandy cove, sheltered by blue clay hills, is a favourite among locals hiking, sunbathing and swimming. A Knight's-era coastal tower adds historic interest to Malta's most naturally beautiful beach.

A Day in Valletta

City Gate. See page 32. Designed by renowned architect Renzo Piano, this is the main entrance to Valletta, flanked by Malta's parliament building. Nearby you'll find Teatru Rjal: an open-air theatre set amidst the ruins of the Royal Theatre destroyed during World War II.

St John's Co-Cathedral. See page 33. This impressive church is the burial place for most of the Grand Masters of the Knights of St John. Breeze through the museum to see the Caravaggio masterpieces.

Museum of Archaeology. See page 33. This sixteenth-century palazzo is home to the priceless artefacts recovered from Malta's ancient Neolithic temples, including the immense "Fat Lady" sculptures.

City Gate

🍴 **Lunch.** See page 42. Soak up the city's atmosphere at *Caffe Cordina*, with lavish interior and pretty *pjazza*.

The Grand Master's Palace. See page 35. The centre of political power from the Knights' era to today dominates the main square.

Fort St Elmo & The National War Museum. See page 39. The site of the most violent battles of the Great Siege, Fort St Elmo is now home to the National War Museum, offering a superb overview of Malta's history.

Barrakka Gardens. See page 26. Offering Valletta's best sunset views over the Grand Harbour.

Caffe Cordina

🍴 **Dinner.** See page 43. *Harbour Club* has perhaps some of the best contemporary-meets-local fare in Malta, and stunning harbour views.

Strait Street. See page 36. The former red-light district spans the length of the city, and is today home to lively bars and restaurants.

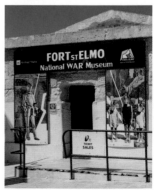

Fort St Elmo and the National War Museum

A Day in Gozo & Comino

Coffee. See page 120. The light Italian fare at *Capitan Spriss* will keep you energized for a day of sightseeing.

The Ċittadella. See page 106. Beautifully preserved, this ancient citadel offers 360-degree views of Gozo's terraced hills and an excellent (free) interpretation centre. Gozo's real attraction lies in its natural beauty, which you'll need the rest of the day to soak up.

Bus Dwejra #311 > Victoria Bus #306 > Xmun

Xlendl. See page 110. A small, extremely picturesque seaside village with turquoise waters sheltered by striking limestone cliffs, with a seaside promenade lined by excellent restaurants.

Lunch. See page 121. The most relaxing restaurant in Xlendi, *Zafiro* specializes in homemade pasta, fresh seafood and lovely sea views.

Bus #306 or 330 > Bus Victoria #311 > Dwejra

Dwejra and the Inland Sea. See page 117. Once home to Malta's natural wonder, the Azure Window (until it fell into the sea in 2017), Dwejra's attraction persists in its wildly beautiful coastal landscape and Inland Sea.

Dbieġi Crafts Village. See page 119. Pick up souvenirs including Maltese lace, local sheep's wool sweaters, silver filigree jewellery, leather goods and ceramics.

Victoria Bus #307 or #322 > Xagħra

Ġgantija temples. See page 112. Gozo's own Neolithic wonder, Ġgantija temples are also among the oldest free-standing structures in human history, pre-dating Stonehenge and Egypt's pyramids.

Xagħra Bus #307 or #322 > Victoria

Cittadella

Xlendi

Dwejra and the Inland Sea

Malta for Families

Although it can be tricky to manoeuvre prams along the narrow streets, Malta is a great destination for families, with plenty of child-friendly attractions and places to explore.

Popeye's Village. See page 89. The set for the 1980 Robin Williams movie is preserved as a small but quaint seaside family fun park.

Mellieħa Bus #223 or #X1 > Ghadira Beach, Mellieħa Bus #221 > Qawra

National Aquarium. See page 82. Get to know the fish you'll encounter while swimming in Malta, as well as a host of tropical visitors including clownfish, rays and tiny sharks.

🍽 **Lunch.** See page 91. *Acqua Marina* is a hidden gem, run by a gracious family, offering simple, authentic, undeniably good Sicilian cuisine.

Bugibba Bus #48 > Floriana Bus #3 > Kalkara

Esplora. See page 52. Malta's National Science Museum, housed in a former British Navy hospital in the Grand Harbour, hosts more than 200 delightful interactive exhibits and a planetarium that appears to levitate within the shell of a World War II damaged palace.

Birgu Bus #1-4 or #21 > Valletta Bus #13, 14, 15 or 16 > Sliema

---

🍽 **Dinner.** See page 62. Fill up on *Bianco's* wood-fired pizzas and generous plates of pasta at this charming, family-friendly seaside restaurant, a local institution.

Evening stroll. See page 54. Along the pretty 5km promenade that stretches from Sliema to St Julian's.

Popeye's Village

National Aquarium

Esplora

Military Malta

Malta has a rich military history, in part due to its central Mediterranean location and the legacy of the Knights of Malta. Here are the major sights not to miss.

Fort St Angelo. See page 50. At the very tip of Birgu's peninsula, dramatic Fort St Angelo's recently restored, tremendously thick fortifications plunge directly into the sea and embody the intimidating military spirit of the Knights.

Fort Rinella. See page 52. Home to a truly massive 100-tonne gun, this volunteer-run fort also offers delightful historic cavalry demonstrations where gentle, retired racehorses steal the show. There is also a café on-site with a seasonal menu.

Valletta fortifications. See page 26. Stroll along Valletta's seashore for an invader's view of its imposing fortifications. A well-worn path begins as you descend the stairs opposite the Sacra Infermeria and ends at the Valletta-Sliema ferry.

Lascaris War Rooms. See page 27. Now with twice daily guided tours offered by kind and knowledgeable volunteers, the Lascaris War Rooms were the secret setting for Malta's disproportionately important role in World War II. Since 2009, the Malta Hertiage Trust has been restoring the complex to provide a welcoming experience for visitors.

Palace Armoury. See page 35. When the Knights departed Malta, they left behind a rich cultural legacy – plus an impressive cache of sixteenth-century armour. The Armoury was first opened to the public in 1860, becoming Malta's first public museum.

Fort St Angelo

Lascaris War Rooms

Palace Armoury

Baroque Malta

Baroque architecture dominates in Malta – from grand churches, decorative palaces and beautiful ornate flourishes on every street, to the dramatic domes that dot the skyline.

Grand Master's Palace State Rooms. See page 35. One of the first buildings constructed in Valletta by Grand Master Jean de Vallette in 1566 after his victory in the Great Siege. You can spend good hours enjoying the frescoes, tapestries and more, here, then sit outside and admire the building from the lovely St George's Square.

St John's Co-Cathedral. See page 33. A dizzying expression of Baroque extravagance, no surface is left untouched by gilding, painting, marble or sculpture. The cathedral is also home to several of Baroque master Caravaggio's best works.

Mdina Cathedral. See page 67. More restrained than its sister cathedral, St John's, St Paul's Cathedral in Mdina is nonetheless impressive and truly atmospheric, and dominates the skyline for miles around.

Maltese balconies. Look up in nearly every street to be rewarded with views of Malta's charming wooden balconies, many in traditional bright colours, believed to be inspired by the Grand Master's Palace's first extravagant examples.

Teatru Manoel. See page 37. Like Malta itself, Teatru Manoel is small but stunning, and can stake a claim as one of Europe's most impressive theatres. Take a 30-minute guided tour or enjoy a full experience by visiting during a scheduled evening performance.

Grand Master's Palace State Rooms

St John's Co-Cathedral Museum

Maltese balconies

Ancient Malta

There is a reason for such a remarkable number of UNESCO World Heritage Sites here – you won't wander far before witnessing Malta's impressive ancient heritage.

Ħaġar Qim and Mnajdra temples. See page 99. These two striking Neolithic temples (older than Egypt's pyramids) sit amongst untouched Maltese countryside. A compelling interpretation centre attempts to unravel their mysteries.

Tarxien temples. See page 94. Nestled amongst residential townhouses, this complex of four megalithic structures dates back to 3600 BCE and is home to some of the best surviving examples of prehistoric art.

Ħal Saflieni Hypogeum. See page 95. Carved into solid limestone more than 6000 years ago, this haunting, beautiful and mysterious underground burial site is not to be missed.

Cart ruts. See page 77. An abundance of ancient, parallel ruts gouged into the limestone surface that lead, inexplicably, off of cliffs or abruptly end; their use is as yet unknown, which adds to their allure.

National Museum of Archaeology. See page 33. A sixteenth-century palazzo home to the bulk of Malta's ancient treasures, this museum provides an overview of the country's ancient history from 5200 to 2500 BCE through artefacts and scholarship.

Ġgantija temples. See page 112. The oldest temples found in the country, local legend holds that these temples were built by a group of giants (not so far-fetched, when you see their size).

Tarxien temples

National Museum of Archaeology

Ġgantija temples

PLACES

Valletta

Valletta

Few leave Valletta (commonly referred to as il-Belt or The City) without falling in love with this tiny capital city, designated in its entirety as a UNESCO World Heritage Site. Valletta – one of Europe's first planned cities – was an impenetrable Baroque capital that is now the centre of Malta's cultural, culinary and commercial life. Immerse yourself in its layers of history, from the late Renaissance to the contemporary, as you scale its many levels – for this is a city of staircases, built unusually short and deep to accommodate the armour-bearing Knights of St John, while a ring of golden limestone fortifications encloses its tight grid of narrow streets full of churches, palaces and townhouses. The outstanding cathedral and Knights' former palace head a list of sights that include Malta's national museums and art galleries. Valletta is also home to a blooming bar and foodie scene.

Auberge de Castille

MAP P.28, POCKET MAP E7
Pjazza Kastilja. Closed to the public.
Dominating Valletta's highest point, the **Auberge de Castille** is the largest and most impressive of Valletta's four surviving *auberges* (historic inns for regional groups of Knights). This monumental

Saluting Battery

Baroque building stands as a reminder of the superiority of the Knights of Castille, one of the brotherhood's largest chapters. Though designed in the 1570s by Girolamo Cassar in the austere style the Knights then preferred, it was rebuilt in grand Baroque style during the eighteenth century to occupy a whole block. The large column-framed doorway is topped with a bust of Grand Master de Fonseca, who initiated the rebuilding. Today, the Auberge de Castille houses the prime minister's office and isn't open to the public, but with two imposing cannons flanking its front door, it's a popular stop for photo opportunities. Linger here long enough and you may even spot a dignitary or two.

Upper Barrakka Gardens and the Saluting Battery

MAP P.28, POCKET MAP E7
Pjazza Kastilja. Free.
Set high behind the ramparts of Valletta's fortifications, this small garden, sprinkled with fragrant

Visiting Valletta

All **buses** to and from Valletta terminate at the bus station outside its main gate. If you're **driving**, avoid entering the city, which is Malta's only controlled vehicle access (CVA) area. An access levy is charged (rental car companies often add their own processing fees to this) and parking is limited – you can avoid the CVA by parking in the multi-storey car park near the bus station (prices vary depending on time, averaging €2/hr). Alternately, use the **park-and-ride service**; the car park, signposted in major approaches to Valletta, is just outside Floriana, and free mini-buses shuttle commuters between here and Valletta's St George's Square, Auberge de Castille or Fort St Elmo every few minutes between 6am and 9pm. From Sliema, a **ferry** makes the 5min journey to Marsamxett on the western flank of Valletta (daily every 30min) and a second ferry travels from Valletta's Barriera Wharf to Birgu (daily every 30min).

There is one infrequent **circular public bus service** inside Valletta's walls, but the city is small enough to see **on foot**. There are also small **electric mini cabs** (akin to golf karts), which operate from 8am to 8pm; flag one down as they pass by or visit the mini-cab stand in front of St John's Co-Cathedral. Next Bike (nextbike.com.mt), a private **bike-rental system**, also has several bicycle stands in Valletta but the city's dramatic hills make it difficult to traverse on two wheels.

flowerbeds, was created in 1661 by the Italian knight Flaminio Balbiani as a retreat for the Knights. Much of it, including its arcaded section, is the original design (the arcaded section was originally roofed, but when Grand Master Ximenes de Texada discovered that dissident Knights were meeting here in 1775 to plot against him, he ordered the roof stripped off as a symbolic warning). The garden still provides a refuge from city bustle and summer heat, but the main reason to visit is for the panoramic view from Valletta's highest point: a vista taking in the breadth of the **Grand Harbour**, including the fantastic medieval townscapes and fortifications of the **Three Cities** (see page 46).

The **Saluting Battery**, accessed from within the garden, spreads over a series of chambers that once served as ammunition stores (☎2180 0992; charge). Today it holds a display of weaponry from the three hundred years it served as an artillery battery for protecting the Grand Harbour, including an anti-aircraft gun that was installed on the terrace in World War II. For history buffs, guided tours are offered on the hour (included in your entrance fee), and two films are shown in rotation: one on the history of "timeguns", and another about the history of the Saluting Battery. At noon and 4pm every day a cannon is fired as a salute – resurrecting a practice dating from the British period.

Lascaris War Rooms

MAP P.28, POCKET MAP E7
Lascaris Ditch; entry either from Girolamo Cassar St or San Anton St (from the latter, follow signs from outside Upper Barakka Gardens) ⓦ lascariswarrooms.com. Charge.
This fascinating (albeit damp) underground complex, gouged deep into the bedrock, was originally used by the Knights as living quarters for their slaves. In

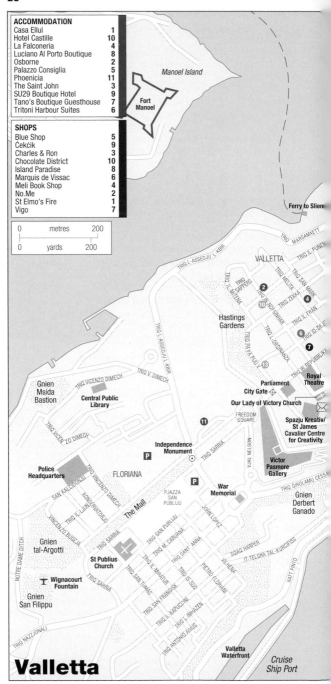

ACCOMMODATION
Casa Ellul	1
Hotel Castille	10
La Falconeria	4
Luciano Al Porto Boutique	8
Osborne	2
Palazzo Consiglia	5
Phoenicia	11
The Saint John	3
SU29 Boutique Hotel	9
Tano's Boutique Guesthouse	7
Tritoni Harbour Suites	6

SHOPS
Blue Shop	5
Čekčik	9
Charles & Ron	3
Chocolate District	10
Island Paradise	8
Marquis de Vissac	6
Meli Book Shop	4
No.Me	2
St Elmo's Fire	1
Vigo	7

Valletta

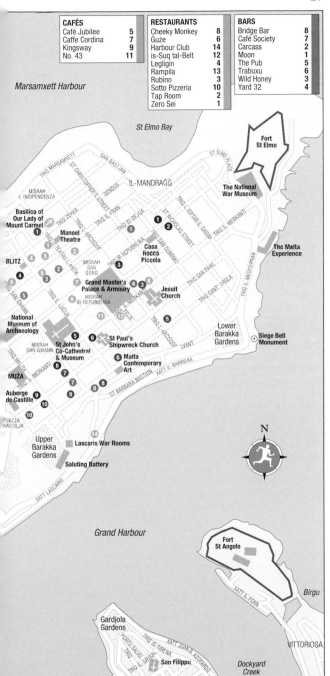

CAFÉS
Café Jubilee	5
Caffe Cordina	7
Kingsway	9
No. 43	11

RESTAURANTS
Cheeky Monkey	8
Ġuże	6
Harbour Club	14
is-Suq tal-Belt	12
Legligin	4
Rampila	13
Rubino	3
Sotto Pizzeria	10
Tap Room	2
Zero Sei	1

BARS
Bridge Bar	8
Café Society	7
Carcass	2
Moon	1
The Pub	5
Trabuxu	6
Wild Honey	3
Yard 32	4

Marsamxett Harbour

St Elmo Bay

Fort St Elmo

IL-MANDRAĠĠ

The National War Museum

MISRAĦ L-INDIPENDENZA

Basilica of Our Lady of Mount Carmel

Manoel Theatre

Casa Roccà Piccola

The Malta Experience

BLITZ

MISRAĦ SAN ĠORG

Grand Master's Palace & Armoury

Jesuit Church

MISRAĦ IR-REPUBBLIKA

National Museum of Archaeology

St John's Co-Cathedral & Museum

St Paul's Shipwreck Church

Malta Contemporary Art

Lower Barakka Gardens

Siege Bell Monument

MUŻA

MISRAĦ SAN ĠWANN

Auberge de Castille

PJAZZA KASTILJA

Upper Barakka Gardens

Lascaris War Rooms

Saluting Battery

N

Grand Harbour

Fort St Angelo

Birgu

XATT IL-FORN

Gardjola Gardens

San Filippu

VITTORIOSA

Dockyard Creek

1940, it was converted into the **Lascaris War Rooms**, the British forces' Maltese centre of operations and the headquarters of the Royal Navy's Mediterranean Fleet during World War II. Conditions were claustrophobic – one thousand people worked here, 240 at a time in six-hour shifts – but it was from Lascaris that the Allies changed the course of World War II in the Mediterranean by severely disrupting the Axis supplies to North Africa, launching the invasion of Sicily, and eventually engineering Italy's surrender. An interesting **museum** now re-creates the wartime atmosphere with wax dummies, maps, props and examples of weaponry such as the J-type Contact Mines that the Italians planted around Malta's seas. Each room is dedicated to an area of operation; the largest concentrates on Operation Husky, the 1943 Allied invasion of Sicily directed by General Dwight Eisenhower, where a large map of Sicily details the multi-pronged attack by air and sea. A **short film** on Malta's wartime experience is shown throughout the day, and an hour underground here gives a good impression of what life must have been like during this tumultuous time. If you have the opportunity, a **tour** with one of the museum's charming

Valletta's renaissance

Visitors may notice an unusual number of **abandoned buildings** in the capital city. In fact, about thirty percent of property is vacant and much of this uninhabitable. During World War II, Valletta sustained heavy damage from aerial bombardments, and then changing social and economic conditions (including the departure of the British navy and most of the city's jobs in the 1960s) led to a mass exodus from the city and, eventually, the whole country. Post-World War II, Valletta earned a reputation for being derelict and unsafe, with most residents living in government-subsidized housing. To put things in perspective, during World War II the city's population was over 23,000 but by 2015 it had plummeted to 6000 (of which more than 25 percent were over 65). Despite this (temporary) decline, in 1980 Valletta was named a UNESCO World Heritage Site as an ideal example of a late Renaissance planned city and its association with the Knights, one of the greatest military forces of modern Europe.

In the last few years, Valletta has undergone a rapid renaissance. Bars, restaurants, shops and hotels breathed new life into the city for its **2018 European Capital of Culture** title. Streets are pedestrianized and public squares have been completely regenerated. Plus, cultural institutions like MUŻA (see page 32) and the Valletta Design Cluster (see page 36) have put Valletta on the map for art and culture lovers. Gradually, younger residents are returning to the city and record numbers of tourists and cruise passengers are discovering its charms. Derelict buildings are fewer, and real-estate prices are skyrocketing in anticipation of the city's complete regeneration. It will be some time before the entire city bustles with life once more, but the tide is turning: Valletta has never been lovelier, with an eclectic blend of new and old at every turn. This is the perfect time to visit.

volunteer guides is worthwhile. Recommended viewing before your visit is *The Malta Story*, a 1950s World War II movie filmed in the Lascaris War Rooms a few years after operations here ceased.

Victor Pasmore Gallery

MAP P.28, POCKET MAP E7
The Polverista, St James Counterguard, Annexe of the Central Bank of Malta
Ⓦ victorpasmoregallery.com. Free.
Located in a *polverista*, or gunpowder magazine, built during the construction of the outer fortification walls of Valletta in the 1640s, the **Victor Pasmore Gallery** features a compact but compelling permanent display of works by British abstract artist Victor Pasmore (1908–98), many produced after his move to the island in 1966.

Spazju Kreattiv/St James Cavalier Centre for Creativity

MAP P.28, POCKET MAP E7
Castille Square Ⓦ kreattivita.org. Charge.
Malta's national centre for modern arts occupies the historic site of **St James Cavalier**, an imposing pentagonal tower built opposite the Auberge de Castille in the 1570s to serve as a rearguard defence position. Within its thick walls sit a series of half-barrel ammunition chambers connected to a ramp that leads to the roof (where heavy guns used to be installed). The complex was converted into an arts centre in 1995 by Richard England, Malta's most famous contemporary architect, and the eleven former ammunition chambers now stage temporary art exhibitions in all media by Maltese and international artists. A small **cinema** screens a rotation of independent films and live opera performances (check the website for schedules). On weekends between October and May, plays, musicals and dance events are also staged in its **theatre-in-the-round**.

Victor Pasmore Gallery

Hastings Gardens

MAP P.28, POCKET MAP D7
Triq Papa Piju V. Free.
Set behind Valletta's fortifications, **Hastings Garden** is dedicated to Lord Hastings, a former British governor who died at sea in 1827 and is buried in the Neoclassical shrine at its centre. The garden's small oaks, pines and shrubs lack appeal, but its lofty viewpoints are reason enough to visit (especially at sunset) – you can see how the Floriana Line fortifications fold over each other to give a 180-degree fire-range; in the moat below, more than a few Hollywood movies have been filmed. Further in the distance, you'll spot Marsamxett Harbour with its yacht marinas, then Manoel Island with its pretty fort and the skylines of urban Sliema and St Julian's. In July, a weekend-long **wine festival** sees this garden come alive with music, local varietals and thirsty crowds (see page 147).

Parliament

City Gate, Parliament and Royal Theatre

The area surrounding Valletta's main entrance, **City Gate**, is proof that Valletta is not a city frozen in time. Designed in 2013 by renowned architect Renzo Piano (famous for the Shard in London and Paris' Centre Pompidou), the sleek and minimalist City Gate comprises a footbridge that crosses an 18m-deep dry moat and passes through the city's ramparts. Entering the city, visitors are confronted with a sweeping view of Malta's Parliament buildings – designed by Piano to appear to levitate above the public square below – and the city's main thoroughfare, **Republic Street**. Both the City Gate and Parliament were constructed entirely of cream-coloured limestone blocks painstakingly installed in the exact order they were extracted from quarries in Gozo – note the delicate pink veins that run across the facade as a result. The innovative design of the **Parliament**'s facade is intended to filter solar radiation while filling the building with natural light, reducing the structure's energy footprint. Adjacent, you'll find

Pjazza Teatru Rjal (the Royal Theatre; ⓦ pjazzateatrurjal.gov. mt), where Piano designed a splendid modern open-air theatre within the ruins of the Royal Opera, a lavish nineteenth-century theatre decimated by World War II bombings. During the summer months, Pjazza Teatru Rjal is an enchanting venue for cultural performances and cinema screenings under the stars (check the website for listings).

MUŻA

MUŻA (*Mużew Nazzjonali tal-Arti*) is Malta's national museum of art, located in the **Auberge d'Italie** on Merchant Street. The building was the seat of the Italian Knights of the Order of St John. MUŻA opened in late 2018 to replace the old Fine Arts Museum (South Street, Valletta). A completely refurbished space three times larger than its predecessor, MUŻA houses an expanded permanent collection of artefacts and works of art. The building was designed to be entirely green-powered and has a carbon-neutral footprint.

Our Lady of Victory Church

MAP P.28, POCKET MAP E7

Triq in-Nofsinhar, Victory Square. Charge.

The first church built in Valletta, the tiny **Our Lady of Victory** was erected to mark the spot where the foundation stone of the city was laid by Grand Master Jean de Valette in 1566. The titular painting behind the main altar, depicting the birth of the Virgin Mary, is said to date to the same period. According to his wishes, La Valette was originally buried here and his coats of arms were painted inside the church. His remains were later transferred to **St John's Co-Cathedral**.

National Museum of Archaeology

MAP P.28, POCKET MAP E7

Republic St Ⓦ heritagemalta.mt. Charge.

Built in 1575 to a design by Girolamo Cassar, the former Auberge de Provence now houses the **National Museum of Archaeology**, with an array of exhibits dating from 5200 to 2500 BCE that represent the legacy of the Neolithic era's most advanced nation. Though the display cases themselves could benefit from a modern facelift, it is well worth spending some time here to learn about the enormity of this little island's ancient history. The sheer size and age of the artefacts here will also hold interest for children.

The collection is exhibited chronologically, starting from 5200–4400 BCE with skeletal remains and some of the earliest artistic representations of humans. The exhibits then describe the discovery of Malta's various **Neolithic temples**, offering theories on how these massive complexes were constructed. There's even a stone model dating from the temple-building period, considered to be the first ever architectural design. The most stirring displays are in the **Human Figure** room, including phallic

stone symbols and a cluster of voluptuous female nudes and sexless figures with pleated skirts and headdresses thought to have been made for ceremonial use. Some of the figures are headless, suggesting that different heads were affixed to the loop at the neck for different ceremonies. The museum's star exhibit, the "**sleeping lady**", is a delicate, hand-sized figurine unearthed from the Hypogeum that depicts a large woman reclining on a couch; carved in minute detail, her body's tranquil pose could be at temporary or eternal rest. The Neolithic floor ends with the dramatic Tarxien Hall, where contents of the 4200-square-metre **Tarxien Temple complex** are exhibited, including megaliths carved with animals, fish and spiral motifs (thought to symbolize a worldview of cyclical continuity) and, more importantly, hollowed altars in which animal bones and flint knives were found – the strongest evidence of animal sacrifices in Malta's temples.

On the upper floor, separate exhibits on **Bronze Age** and **Phoenician** artefacts present mostly pottery and funerary art, with an interesting section dedicated to Malta's **cart ruts** (see page 77). The remainder of the upper floor comprises several ornate and elaborately decorated palace rooms that house temporary exhibitions.

St John's Co-Cathedral and Museum

MAP P.28, POCKET MAP E7

St John St Ⓦ stjohnscocathedral.com. Charge.

Don't let its austere facade fool you – stepping inside **St John's Co-Cathedral** is like entering a brilliant jewellery box. The Cathedral was designed by Girolamo Cassar in 1570 as the conventual church of the Order, replacing St Lawrence Church in Birgu (see page 48). In the

The Ċittadella

latter half of the seventeenth century the Knights set about transforming the plain interior of the cathedral – dedicated to the Order's patron saint – into a blaze of Baroque art. The Calabrian artist Mattia Preti (1613–99) supervised the twenty-year project, which in some years cost more than Malta's entire military budget. Most of the artworks in the cavernous nave are the work of Preti, who was also responsible for several of the altar paintings.

The **nave** of the cathedral is overwhelmingly sumptuous. Pillars are ablaze with mesmerizing gold and blue leaf carvings and representations of the Maltese Cross, while the eighteen vignettes on the vault, depicting episodes from St John's life, took Preti five years to complete (painting directly onto the concave ceiling, he had to tinker carefully with the perspective so that the view from the ground wouldn't be distorted). The floor of the nave, meanwhile, has 364 inlaid marble tombs of influential Knights: each features a Latin eulogy and epitaph framed by symbols of prestige and glory.

The artistic diversity of the Co-Cathedral was further enhanced when **eight side-chapels** were individually assigned to each *langue*, or Knightly regional grouping, which competed to create the most flamboyant decoration (you'd be hard pressed to pick a winner, though the Chapel of the Langue of Aragon would certainly be in the running). To the right of the chancel in the chapel dedicated to Our Lady of Carafa, Grand Master La Vallette is interred in a stone sarcophagus; this is the only part of the church that retains its original monastic simplicity (La Vallette would have been pleased).

Departing the nave, visitors enter the **Oratory of St John**, which holds the cathedral's most valuable relic: the *Beheading of St John the Baptist*, **Caravaggio**'s magnificent masterpiece painted in 1608. A stunning achievement for its time, many art historians consider it the best painting of the seventeenth century given its grim realism, excellent composition and virtuoso use of light and shade. The second Caravaggio on display, *St Jerome Writing*, is a less dramatic but deeply human work. The oratory itself – full of dense carvings and motifs – is also the work of Preti.

Beyond the oratory, a **museum** showcases the church's moveable art: heaps of silverware and vestments, various portraits of Knights and three huge and majestic Flemish tapestries dating from 1702 (these were formerly hung in the Co-Cathedral's nave). The museum is still undergoing a total refurbishment and extension project, which started in 2016, to accommodate increasing visitor numbers. Note that high heels are banned in the interest of preserving the nave's intricate tombs (slippers can be purchased). Women must cover their shoulders (free shawls are provided) and visitor numbers are limited to 52 persons in the Oratory at a time.

St Paul's Shipwreck Church

MAP P.28, POCKET MAP E7
St Paul St ☎ 2123 6013. Free.

The capital's most opulent church after the Co-Cathedral, **St Paul's** is dedicated to the shipwreck of Malta's favourite saint in 60 AD (see page 84). The present structure, consecrated in 1740, is the third incarnation on this site and its rich and dense interior is awash in crimson and gold. Closer inspection reveals silver chandeliers and statues of the Apostles, ornate altars in the side-chapels, and numerous memorials to St Paul including a fragment of the saint's wrist bone set in a gilded reliquary and the pillar on which he was beheaded. This church celebrates its feast twice a year (Feb 10 and June 29, both public holidays) with lively, elaborate parades.

St George's Square

MAP P.28, POCKET MAP E6
Republic St.

Valletta's main square, flanked by the Grand Master's Palace and an Italian Cultural Institute, is the site for most of Malta's national celebrations and events, including Carnival, New Year's Eve, Malta Arts Festival and Malta Fashion Week (🌐fashionweek.com.mt). The fountain puts on a musical show hourly throughout the day, set against the regal *Malta Suite* score by composer Charles Camilleri. A monument here commemorates the events of Sette Giugno (June 7, 1919), when British troops fired into a crowd of people protesting increasing living costs in this square, killing four.

Summer nights in St George's Square are particularly lovely, as locals pour into the square to escape the heat of their flats and children splash about in the fountain. Passing through the square, take note of the impressive green balconies that wrap around the corners of the Grand Master's Palace – these are thought to be the inspiration for many of the ubiquitous Maltese balconies of today.

Grand Master's Palace and Armoury

MAP P.28, POCKET MAP E7
Republic St, St George's Square. Charge.

An imposing two-storey building occupying an entire block, the **Grand Master's Palace** served as Malta's seat of political power from 1571, when it was designed by Girolamo Cassar for the Knights, to 2015, when Parliament was moved to its new home designed by Renzo Piano (see page 32). Today, it is home to the Office of the President of Malta and five of its grand rooms are open for the public to explore. Perhaps the most compelling part of the palace is the handsome corridor that connects these rooms, richly decorated with marble floors depicting the Grand Master's coats of arms and painted from floor to ceiling with a series of lunettes depicting Knightly naval battles. Adjoining State Rooms feature dramatic, thick-coffered and panelled timber ceilings with gilding, massive chandeliers and portraits of various Grand Masters (who each modified and embellished the palace during their tenure).

The **Throne Room** was used by Grand Masters to host ambassadors and high-ranking dignitaries; the President of Malta continues to use the room for the same purpose today. The frescoes in this room were painted by 1576 by the Italian Matteo Perez D'Aleccio and depict key events of the Knights' history. The **Council Room** (where the ruling council, akin to today's government cabinet, held its meetings) is adorned with three-hundred-year-old copies of the fantastic Gobelin Tapestries, depicting romanticized scenes of New World animals and hunters encountered by the German Prince Johan Mauritz of Nassau during his expedition from 1636 to 1644. The **State Dining Room**, rebuilt after being hit during a World War II air raid, features portraits of Maltese Heads of State since the country achieved its independence in 1964. The **Page's Waiting Room** is connected to the Grand Master's private apartments (disappointingly, not open to the public) and the frescoes here describe scenes from the Knights' history before they arrived in Malta. In the adjoining and richly crimson **Hall of Ambassadors** the fresco series continues, with the addition of Baroque portraits of Grand Masters.

On the ground floor, the absorbing **Palace Armoury** was opened to the public in 1860 as Malta's first public museum. One of the world's largest collections and the most visible and tangible symbol of the order's military glories, the armoury spreads over two barrel-vaulted halls that were originally used as the palace stables. The first room now displays armour and the second a mass of weaponry, including swords, muskets, cannons and crossbows. The Knights had enough military hardware to equip an army of 18,000 and although only a fraction of this haul remains, the 5000 or so pieces on display are representative of virtually the whole range of armaments produced between the sixteenth and eighteenth centuries in Malta and other European countries. The highlight of the Armoury is undoubtedly the priceless damascened suit of body armour that belonged to Grand Master Wignacourt, entirely encrusted in gold and silver fleur-de-lys and military symbols.

Il-Mandraġġ
MAP P.28, POCKET MAP F6

Occupying the northern corner of Valletta, the former slum district of **Il-Mandraġġ** is demarcated on two sides by the sea, and on the other two by Old Theatre Street and Strait Street. Until the 1960s, the area's alleys were densely populated and alive with the activity of blacksmiths, butchers, bakers and bars. Il-Mandraġġ was described in the 1930s by British writer Evelyn Waugh as "the most concentrated and intense slum in the world". This sentiment, unfortunately, has persisted locally, giving il-Mandraġġ a reputation as a rough and dangerous area. Today, the reality is quite the opposite. Crumbling stone buildings towering over narrow alleys remain faithful to the original urban fabric of Valletta, and are slowly being regenerated into refurbished flats, artist studios and boutique hotels. Malta's national design centre, the **Valletta Design Cluster**, is also located here.

It's worth exploring this rapidly changing area to absorb the atmosphere of the "real" Valletta (*il-Belt*) that lies beyond the city's pristine palazzos. The area is safe, and scratching the surface reveals a close-knit community who are "Beltin first, Maltese second". If you really want to step off the beaten path, descend through the **Jew's Sally Port** at the end of St Nicholas Street for a taste of local life; here, fighting for space on the seashore, you'll find a concentration of tumbledown shanties where families gather on hot summer evenings for languid barbeques.

The Gut
MAP P.28, POCKET MAP E7

This narrow section of lower Strait Street, nicknamed "**The Gut**" by British sailors, is Valletta's former red-light district. For virtually all of Valletta's history, the area was populated with a combination of small bars, taverns, music halls and brothels, but its heyday was from the 1920s to the 1960s when sex workers, drag queens and jazz musicians entertained British and American sailors here. Independence in 1964 caused a steep decline in the number of visiting servicemen, and from the 1970s most of Strait Street closed down, to be abandoned and unloved for the next forty years. The awarding to Valletta of the 2018 European Capital of Culture title sparked a renewed interest in the area and today The Gut is at the centre of Malta's most exciting bar and restaurant scene, with several establishments, such as *Silver Horse* (see page 44), restored to their former glory. As you wander along this narrow alley, look for the **original signs** for bars and music halls, miraculously still in situ. Most food and drink establishments are located at the intersection of Strait Street and Old Theatre Street, though *Yard 32* (see page 45) and *Trabuxu* (see page 45) – located in the historically more gentrified area of upper Strait Street, which was frequented by more senior Navy officers – are also worth seeking out. On weekends during the summer, live musicians perform up and down the street.

Manoel Theatre

MAP P.28, POCKET MAP E6

115 Old Theatre St ⓦ teatrumanoel.mt. Charge.

Malta's national theatre and home of the Malta Philharmonic Orchestra, the **Manoel Theatre** (Teatru Manoel) is one of Europe's oldest and most impressive. Personally funded by Grand Master Antonio Manoel de Vilhena in 1731 "for the honest recreation of the people" (which is inscribed above the main entrance to the theatre), it is wholly built from timber with an intimate six-hundred-seat oval-shaped interior ringed by boxes, topped by an elegant pale-blue-and-gold trompe l'oeil ceiling. Two reservoirs

underground perfect the acoustics, which are so precise that orchestral conductors have to work from one side of the stage to prevent the rustle made by turning the pages of music sheets being audible in the auditorium. Half-hour **guided tours** outline the construction of the theatre and its history, but the Manoel is best appreciated during evening performances (see page 143).

Basilica of Our Lady of Mount Carmel

MAP P.28, POCKET MAP E6

Old Theatre St. Free.

The looming dome of the **Basilica of Our Lady of Mount Carmel**, together with the spire of the nearby **St John's Anglican Cathedral**, are the iconic features of Valletta's skyline. Following its destruction in World War II, the rebuilding of the basilica (the original dated from the 1570s) took twenty years and demonstrated a reassertion of the dominance of Baroque architecture in Malta. The resulting structure shows more concern with size than it does with artistic detail; the interior of

Manoel Theatre

the church is uncharacteristically restrained, while the egg-shaped dome attempts to eclipse its neighbour.

Blitz

MAP P.28, POCKET MAP E6
St Lucy St 68 ⓦ blitzvalletta.com.

Blitz is an independent, not-for-profit contemporary-arts project space situated in a four-level, four-hundred-year-old Valletta townhouse. Its unique setting and excellent temporary exhibitions make it worth a visit; check the website for listings.

Casa Rocca Piccola

MAP P.28, POCKET MAP F6
74 Republic St ⓦ casaroccapiccola.com.
Charge including guided tour.

Casa Rocca Piccola is a private sixteenth-century palazzo owned and operated by a noble Maltese family; their ancestor Cosimo de Piro left Rhodes in the general exodus of the Knights of St John in 1530. The palazzo's current inhabitants, the Marquis Nicholas de Piro and his wife Frances, were the first members of the Maltese aristocracy to open their house to the public, offering visitors a glimpse of what must lie beyond the palatial facades of Valletta's other palazzos. Highlights include an underground cistern turned World War II shelter, a chatty pet parrot named Kiko and a delightful collection of local contemporary and historic art.

Valletta Contemporary

MAP P.28, POCKET MAP F7
15–17 East St ⓦ vallettacontemporary.com.
Free.

Founded in 2018, Malta's foremost **contemporary art gallery** hosts an engaging and diverse programme of exhibitions and events. The gallery was the brainchild of Norbert Francis Attard, a painter, poster-maker and installation artist, and exhibits reflect his multi-disciplinary approach. Check the gallery's website for current exhibition listings.

Jesuit Church

MAP P.28, POCKET MAP F7
Merchant St.

The **Jesuit Church** is one of the oldest in Valletta, built between 1592 and 1609 with an originally plain facade that was redesigned by famous Baroque architect Francesco Buonamici in 1647. The interior is uniquely serene by Maltese standards, with a delicate buttery yellow colour and restrained Doric architectural influences. Its oratory invites further exploration, a tiny room with a candy-coloured ceiling and an overwhelming profusion of paintings, sculpture and marble that more than compensate for the restraint of the church proper. The adjacent Jesuit College, built concurrently, is today the **University of Malta's** Valletta campus.

Lower Barrakka Gardens

MAP P.28, POCKET MAP F7
East St. Free.

A Tranquil Star by Anthea Hamilton and Nicholas Byrne, Malta Contemporary Art

Located at the tip of Valletta's peninsula, **Lower Barrakka Gardens** are the counterpoint to their sister, Upper Barrakka (see page 26). Slightly smaller but no less attractive, visitors can admire views from the Grand Harbour here under the shade of olive trees. With a cheerful pub and casual kiosk flanking its entrance, Lower Barrakka Gardens is also a popular meeting place for locals. Enjoy a local lager here while taking in a splendid taste of life in *il-Belt*.

Siege Bell Monument

MAP P.28, POCKET MAP F7
Mediterranean St. Free.

This huge **bell**, mounted on a specially built podium, was erected in 1992 and jointly inaugurated by the then Maltese President Ċensu Tabone and Queen Elizabeth II to commemorate the anniversary of the George Cross Award to Malta (see page 39) and to honour the seven thousand servicemen, women and civilians who died here during World War II. The bell tolls daily at noon, and its boom – intended as a reminder of Malta's war victims – can be heard throughout Valletta. A visit also offers panoramic harbour views.

Fort St Elmo and the National War Museum

MAP P.28, POCKET MAP F6
St Elmo Place ⓦ heritagemalta.mt. Charge.

Fort St Elmo stands guard at the end of the Sciberras Peninsula on which Valletta is built, erected by the Knights in six months during 1552 in preparation for an imminent invasion by the Turks. Its star shape was intended to provide a defence umbrella of crossfire, and the design undoubtedly worked – St Elmo withstood four weeks of cannon fire from three sides before being captured in the first thrust of the Great Siege of 1565. Later, when Valletta was built, the fort was incorporated within the city's fortifications, and during the

seventeenth century the **Carafa Enceinte** was built enclosing the original fort.

Today, the **Rampart** is open to the public for free and is the access point for the restored fortress. Malta's marvellous **National War Museum**, perhaps the best museum in Malta and an essential part of any visit to Valletta, is set within the inner fort. To access the museum, cross the fortress's beautiful inner courtyard before ascending a small staircase to the fort's upper level. Absorbing, interactive exhibits, spread across five halls, take visitors on a journey through Malta's history, which, from the Bronze Age to World War II, was dramatically shaped by military conflict. Highlights include Roosevelt's "Husky" Jeep and "Faith", the sole survivor of the three Gloster Gladiator biplanes that performed so bravely in Malta's air defences in 1939. The 1942 George Cross award, given to Malta for its endurance during the intense aerial bombing campaign and blockade that pushed the island to the brink of surrender, is also prominently displayed.

The small but handsome **Chapel of St Anne**, built in 1572 and attributed to Gerolamo Cassar, who also designed the Grand Master's Palace, is worth visiting before your departure. It is roofed by a fine barrel-vaulted ceiling with square coffers and deep mouldings.

The Malta Experience and Sacra Infermeria tour

MAP P.28, POCKET MAP F6
Mediterranean Conference Centre, Hospital St ⓦ themaltaexperience.com. Charge.

The **Malta Experience** is a 45-minute film that tells the story of Malta's seven-thousand-year history, making it a popular first stop for visitors to Valletta. Entry includes a tour of the **Sacra Infermeria** (Holy Infirmary), located across the street, which is best visited after you've picked up some knowledge

St Publius Parish Church

of Malta's history from the film. While the Knights are famous for repelling an invasion and their various military exploits, they were founded to care for the sick: it is this part of their history that is revealed at the Sacra Infermeria, built in 1574. Once considered amongst the best hospitals in Europe, the Sacra Infermeria could accommodate more than nine hundred patients in an emergency. Its breathtaking main ward – 155m in length with soaring limestone ribbed vaults – was the longest in Europe at the time, and continued to serve as a Station Hospital until after World War I.

Floriana

MAP P.28, POCKET MAP D7

Floriana was created as – and still very much is – a suburb of Valletta, all modest gardens and grids of residential homes. Blink as you enter Valletta by bus and you might miss it, but linger a little longer and you'll notice the village's monuments (look for a golden eagle atop a pillow commemorating RAF victims of World War II) and its massive town square, **Pjazza San Publiju** (Saint Publius Square), so named for its looming church. Frequently the site of open-air concerts and operas during the summer months, Pjazza San Publiju is also commonly referred to as *Il-Fosos* (The Granaries), as it is here that the Knights dug a series of underground chambers to store enough grain to last two years in the event of an invasion and blockade. Today, the stone caps of the now-sealed chambers are still visible across the square.

The Floriana Lines

In the 1630s, as the Turks expanded their fleet, the Knights feared a second siege and commissioned Pietro Paolo Floriani (engineer to the pope) to assess Malta's defences. Floriani proposed a line of fortifications across the neck of the Sciberras Peninsula – enclosing Valletta and in effect creating a new fortified suburb, Floriana – so that Malta's entire population could be crammed behind the defences in the event of an invasion. In 1670, the defences were strengthened by means of the Floriana Hornwork, a bulwark jutting out from the Lines' southwest corner, with a fire-range extending across the inner creeks of the Grand Harbour. The Floriana Hornwork and **Portes Des Bombes**, the sole gate through the fortifications, were completed in 1716. The **Floriana Lines** proved the ultimate deterrent: the Turks never attacked, in part because of the virtual impossibility of breaking through the impenetrable fortifications. The handsome Portes Des Bombes is today the primary vehicular entry point to Floriana and Valletta beyond.

Shops

Blue Shop

MAP P.28, POCKET MAP E7

37 Merchants St ⓦ blueshopvalletta.com.
With an enviable location on the side of St John's Co-Cathedral, this ladies' fashion boutique specializes in beachy handmade linen dresses and vintage-inspired jewellery.

Ċekċik

MAP P.28, POCKET MAP E7

15 Melita St ⓦ cekcik.com.mt.
A quirky independent shop with a unique collection of vintage items, ceramics, locally designed clothing, original artwork and beautiful postcards.

Charles & Ron

MAP P.28, POCKET MAP E6

58D Republic St ⓦ charlesandron.com.
The flagship store of Maltese haute-couture fashion designers Charles & Ron, where you'll find their latest collection of high-end clothing and handbags with distinctly Maltese imagery and patterns.

Chocolate District

MAP P.28, POCKET MAP E6

13 Melita St ⓦ chocolatedistrict.com
An attractive, vaulted-ceilinged shop selling all manner of artistically-presented treats made from rich Maltese chocolate – salted caramel Easter eggs, dark chocolate halva, bars infused with hops and orange, and a whole lot more.

Island Paradise

MAP P.28, POCKET MAP E7

18 Merchants St
ⓦ islandparadiseboutique.com.
This charming boutique, as its name suggests, specializes in goods which evoke the best sides of island living. The clothing range (women's only) includes floaty sundresses and boho jewellery, while soy candles and rustic-chic homeware are also on offer.

Marquis de Vissac

MAP P.28, POCKET MAP E7

169 St Lucia St ⓦ facebook.com/marquisdevissacespadrille.
Dedicated to handmade espadrilles (unisex, flat wedges) including the rare French Bayona brand, which is only stocked in two shops in the world.

Meli Book Shop

MAP P.28, POCKET MAP E6

185 Old Bakery St ☎ 2123 7266.
A tiny independent bookshop that looks to have come straight out of the 1960s, with an excellent stock of new fiction titles and a vast selection of books about Malta and Maltese-language literature.

No.Me

MAP P.28, POCKET MAP F6

91B Republic St
ⓦ facebook.com/nomestudiovalletta.

Ċekċik

A contemporary Italian design shop that upcycles discarded items into clothing, furniture, jewellery and homeware. The shop's distinctly styled interior is lovely enough to be mistaken for an art gallery.

St Elmo's Fire

MAP P.28, POCKET MAP E6
15–17 East St ☎ 35621251112.

Lovely longstanding boutique specializing in silver jewellery, with Maltese crosses, delicate necklaces and rings, and a friendly owner who will demonstrate how, for example, filigreed silver is made.

Vigo

MAP P.28, POCKET MAP E7
68-9 South St
ⓦ facebook.com/vigovalletta.

Dapper gents will love this independent boutique with unique men's apparel, leather goods, accessories and grooming products.

Cafés

Café Jubilee

MAP P.28, POCKET MAP E6
125 St Lucia St ⓦ cafejubilee.com.

There's an intimate atmosphere at long-established vintage-styled brasserie *Café Jubilee*, so you might just catch bits of gossip from Valletta's politicians, lawyers and police – the national Law Courts are a stone's throw away. Tuck into Nanna's ravioli – you won't find the *dentex* (white fish), lemon and artichoke variety anywhere else – but save room for an authentic Maltese *imqaret* (date-filled pastry) afterwards. €€

Caffe Cordina

MAP P.28, POCKET MAP E6
244 Republic St ⓦ caffecordina.com.

The 180-year-old, family-run *Caffe Cordina* is a Valletta institution. Service is slow, prices inflated and food mostly average, but it's worth stopping by for

a coffee and cake; the tables in front of the National Library are a beautiful spot to watch the world go by, and the interior is richly decorated with paintings by celebrated twentieth-century Maltese painter Giuseppe Cali. €€

Kingsway

MAP P.28, POCKET MAP E7
57 Republic St ⓦ kingswayvalletta.com.

Of all of the cafés surrounding the National Library, *Kingsway* is a standout, offering a unique vibe that nods to Valletta's 1930s heyday. With good coffee and fresh croissants, it's an ideal place for a light breakfast, and there's a small menu of well-priced lunch options that changes daily. Free wi-fi. €

No. 43

MAP P.28, POCKET MAP E7
43 Merchants St
ⓦ facebook.com/no43valletta.

Run by an Australian and Italian husband-and-wife team who relocated to Malta from Florence, *No. 43* is one of Malta's best lunch spots, consistently delivering on its promise of fresh, affordable and healthy food. The menu of anything-but-boring salads and sandwiches changes daily. At midday, expect a queue; if you don't manage to get a table, nearby Upper Barrakka gardens (see page 26) makes a great place for a picnic. €

Restaurants

Cheeky Monkey

MAP P.28, POCKET MAP E7
174 Merchants St
ⓦ cheekymonkeymalta.com.

This popular gastropub is always a safe bet for some hearty grub in a buzzing atmosphere, with big juicy burgers, excellent fish and chips, and a selection of pasta and risotto. There's a good range of beers, too, and sport on the big screen. €€

Ġuże

MAP P.28, POCKET MAP E6
22 Old Bakery St Ⓦ guzebistro.com.

Ask any Maltese person for a restaurant recommendation in Valletta and they are likely to say simply: *Ġuże*. And with good reason: located in a charming sixteenth-century building on Old Bakery Street, the well-priced menu here changes seasonally with a focus on local ingredients; expect dishes such as calamari with almonds and lime and local rabbit with leek and cabbage stuffing. It's best to book in advance as the restaurant's popularity means they can rarely accept walk-ins. €€€

Harbour Club

MAP P.28, POCKET MAP E7
5 Barriera Wharf
Ⓦ theharbourclubmalta.com.

Located at Barriera Wharf, *Harbour Club*'s breathtaking views and small but superb menu makes it a popular choice among locals for long, leisurely meals. The kitchen offers consistently outstanding local fish and handmade pasta, while the pork served three ways is a lovely contemporary homage to the Maltese *majjalata* (pig roast) tradition. In the summer, dinner is served outside; in the winter months the dining room is a one-of-a-kind interior: a breathtaking underground cistern. Bookings are necessary on weekends. €€€

is-Suq tal-Belt

MAP P.28, POCKET MAP E7
Merchants St Ⓦ issuqtalbelt.com.

is-Suq tal-Belt (The City Market) has been restored to its Victorian-era glory, and is the only wrought iron and timber structure in Valletta. A historic site in its own right, visit for the views and stay for the food. Spread over three floors are cafés, an upscale supermarket and a plethora of food stalls offering everything from fresh pasta and wood-fired pizza to Spanish tapas and sushi. Price varies depending on the choice of restaurant/café or food stall. €–€€€

Legligin

MAP P.28, POCKET MAP E6
119 Santa Lucia St Ⓦ legliginmalta.com.

This charming fifteen-table French-Mediterranean restaurant does not have a menu; patrons pay a reasonable fixed price per head for a multiple-course meal of whatever is fresh and in season (expect soups, wonderful breads and dips, fresh fish and stewed octopus). Wash it all down with one of an array of wines – *legligin* is the Maltese word for the *glug-glug-glug* sound of a generous pour. €€€

Rampila

MAP P.28, POCKET MAP E7
1 St John's Cavalier
Ⓦ facebook.com/rampila.

Open for lunch and dinner, *Rampila* is set within Valletta's walls in a romantic vaulted limestone tunnel. The cuisine emphasizes rustic Maltese local specialties like

Inside is-Suq tal-Belt

rabbit *tortellaci* (stuffed pasta) and *bragioli* (thin slices of beef stuffed with egg, beef and minced pork). In the summer, request a table in the pretty garden that overlooks Valletta's City Gate. €€

Rubino

MAP P.28, POCKET MAP E6
53 Old Bakery St Ⓦ rubinomalta.com.
The best place on the island for modestly priced but well-executed local cuisine. The menu is changed every few days, and recurrent seasonal dishes include ox tongue with aubergines and capers, spaghetti with sea urchins, and the dessert *cassata siciliana*, a lovely Italian cheesecake. €€

Sotto Pizzeria

MAP P.28, POCKET MAP E7
32 South St Ⓦ zeroseimalta.com.
Sotto, like its sister restaurant *Zero Sei* (see below), offers hearty Italian cuisine and hospitality. It's an authentic family-run affair specializing in wood-fired pizzas made with dough that leavens for 72 hours. If pizza isn't for you, the pasta and salads are also good. €€

Tap Room

MAP P.28, POCKET MAP E6
53 Old Theatre St Ⓦ taproomvalletta.com.
This hip restaurant offers consistently good food and service. The mussels in cream and champagne are highly recommended, while the salads, pasta and risottos are all thoroughly satisfying. Surprisingly, given its name, *Tap Room* doesn't serve many beers, but it does offer an excellent selection of wines (including high-quality labels) by the glass. €€

Zero Sei

MAP P.28, POCKET MAP E6
75 Old Theatre St Ⓦ zeroseimalta.com.
Located across from the Manoel Theatre, *Zero Sei* is an authentic Roman restaurant where carbonara (including a vegetarian version) is the house speciality. The menu offers excellent value for money. Booking a table here can be difficult; enquire in advance. €€

Bars

Bridge Bar

MAP P.28, POCKET MAP E7
258 St Ursula St
Ⓦ facebook.com/www.bridgebar.valletta.
This place is all about the atmosphere and is especially popular on summer nights, when there can be hundreds jostling for space. If you want a table, book ahead; otherwise join the jovial crowds sitting on the steps. Taking its name from the bridge it is located on, which spans Easat Street above Victoria Gate, *Bridge Bar* offers live jazz on Fridays under a canopy of bougainvillea and stars (weather permitting).

Café Society

MAP P.28, POCKET MAP E7
13 St John St
Ⓦ facebook.com/cafesocietyuptown.
A hip hole-in-the-wall favoured by Malta's artistic set, *Café Society* offers excellent craft beer and cocktails in a quaint, intimate setting. Seating extends onto the steps on St John's Street: a picturesque setting for watching the moon rise over Birgu's fortifications across the Grand Harbour. In the summer, film screenings are also hosted here.

Carcass

MAP P.28, POCKET MAP E7
56 Strait St Ⓦ carcass.com.mt.
Despite the rather grisly name, *Carcass* is one of the liveliest spots in town, self-consciously reviving Strait Street's erstwhile rock 'n' roll reputation with a vintage music soundtrack and some excellent but well-priced cocktails.

Moon

MAP P.28, POCKET MAP E6
93-94 Strait St ☏ 2780 2933.

Under the same ownership as nearby Korean restaurant *Sun*, *Moon* is prominent among the bars housed in restored historic buildings in The Gut, the historically most dangerous and sleazy part of Strait Street and its former red-light district. This laid-back bar offers expertly mixed cocktails amid a brightly-lit, slightly boho décor.

The Pub

MAP P.28, POCKET MAP F6
136 Archbishop St ☎ 7905 2522.
A family-run, English-style pub famed for being the location where British actor Oliver Reed died in 1999 after a heavy drinking session during the making of his last film, *Gladiator*. Occasionally hosts free Shakespeare performances and live-music nights.

Trabuxu

MAP P.28, POCKET MAP E7
2 Strait St ⓦ trabuxu.com.mt.
A wine bar set in an atmospheric old cellar that attracts a laidback Maltese crowd for its selection of 260 wines – prices start at a modest sum

for a mid-range Maltese Cabernet Sauvignon. Tuck into one of the various platters while jazz and blues music flutters in the background.

Wild Honey

MAP P.28, POCKET MAP E6
127 St Lucia St
ⓦ facebook.com/WildHoneyValletta.
An eclectic, relaxed Italian bar serving a variety of craft beers, cocktails and wines. A small but consistently exceptional menu of cheese platters and salads makes this a popular place for couples and groups of friends.

Yard 32

MAP P.28, POCKET MAP E7
32 Strait St ⓦ yard32.com.
Run by Italians who came to Malta by way of Spain, this tapas and gin bar is one of Malta's best. Knowledgeable staff help patrons select one of two hundred gins and forty tonics, perfectly complemented by a variety of tapas. Live music is offered throughout the week, and a gin-themed aquarium makes this bar lovably quirky.

Trabuxu

The Three Cities

Occupying two narrow peninsulas on the other side of the Grand Harbour from Valletta, and enclosed on the land side by Malta's largest defensive fortification, the Three Cities – Birgu, Isla and Bormla – retain a romantic, medieval urban fabric that makes them a pleasure to explore on foot. Atmospheric Birgu has the highest concentration of individual attractions, tucked among winding alleys lined with the residents' informal kerbside gardens. Isla and Bormla both sustained heavy damage during World War II and have no traditional "sights", though a walk along the picturesque promenade from Birgu's marina to Isla offers a lively taste of local life – don't miss the opportunity for a fresh seafood lunch at il-Ħnejja (see page 53). It's also worth strolling just beyond the Three Cities to Kalkara, where Malta's national science museum, Esplora, is located in a British-era quarantine hospital.

Birgu

MAP P.48, POCKET MAP F8

When the Knights arrived in Malta in 1530, the island's capital city, Mdina, did not suit their naval activities and **Birgu** was elected as the site of their stronghold. The city was hastily fortified and **Fort St Angelo** constructed in anticipation of an impending attack by the Ottoman Empire, which duly arrived in 1565 with the Great Siege, during which the new fortress played a key role (see page 50). After the Great Siege, when reinforcements from Sicily caused the Ottomans to abandon their attack, the Knights began planning a new capital city on Mount Sciberras. When their convent and operations were

relocated to Valletta in 1571, Birgu lost its political importance but continued to operate as a naval base for various occupying forces over the following four centuries. During World War II, several of its key historic attractions were destroyed by bombs, but the city remains endearingly charming.

The best way to explore Birgu is on foot. Enter through the **Three Gates** and get lost in the charming **Collachio**. The **Inquisitor's Palace and Maritime Museum** are worth brief interludes. Wander along the city's ramparts and make your way to its harbourfront promenade, which extends from **Fort St Angelo** through the city's new **superyacht marina**. Undoubtedly the most memorable and magical

So nice they named them twice

Perhaps owing to their early history (Birgu was the first village settled by the Knights of Malta), the Three Cities are unique in being commonly referred to each by two names: Birgu (Vittoriosa), Isla (Senglea) and Bormla (Cospicua). We use the (more popular) Maltese names in this book.

time to visit the city is **Birgufest** (see page 147).

The Three Gates and Malta At War Museum

MAP P.48, POCKET MAP G9

Until the Three Cities' fortifications were breached for vehicular access, the grandiose, three-tiered **Three Gates** provided the sole entrance to Birgu and they are still the most picturesque way to enter the city. The **Advanced Gate** is the first, designed in 1722 by French architect François de Mondion, also mastermind of the Magisterial Palace in Mdina (see page 66) and Fort Manoel (see page 58). Just beyond the Advanced Gate you will find the **Malta at War Museum** (⊕ maltaatwarmuseum. com; charge), which offers an excellent overview of what life was like in Malta during World War II, when the island was more heavily bombed in just one week than London was in the entire Blitz: as many as 100,000 people were displaced within Malta during the war, which destroyed 35,000 homes (the subsequent housing shortage persisted until the 1970s). The museum entrance fee includes an audioguide, free guided tours, a short film screening and access to a fascinating underground air-raid shelter: this network of tunnels and small rooms dug into the city's bastion walls includes a surgical ward and birthing room. Within a year and a half, sufficient shelters had been dug into Malta's limestone bedrock to protect the entire island's population.

Opposite the museum is a staircase leading to the **Foss Birgu**, a park in the city's dry moat with mature almond trees and a small, meandering path. Continuing past the museum takes you over a bridge spanning the moat and through the **Couvre Porte Gate**, the second of the three, which opens into a bare stone courtyard from which centuries' old stairs lead to the

Isla (Senglea) Marina

ramparts; at the top you get a good view of the complex fortifications. Across this courtyard is the third **Main Gate**; on the other side is Birgu's main village road.

The Collachio

MAP P.48, POCKET MAP G9

Home base of the Knights between 1530 and 1571, the ancient **Collachio** quarter is a perfect place to lose yourself for an hour on a warm afternoon, characterized by pedestrianized, winding alleys that teem with potted plants; the Knights' earliest Baroque townhouses or *auberges* still survive along Triq Hilda Tabone and Triq Il-Majjistral (all have been converted into public buildings or private residences). Historically, the Collachio played witness to the birth of Malta's first Carnival in 1535; the celebrations marking the end of the Great Siege of 1565; and the frequent march of slaves towards Birgu's main square, where regular auctions were once held – slave labour contributed to the building of the Knight's fortifications and persisted in Malta until Napoleon's arrival in 1798. Note the buildings constructed in a

1950s modernist style: they're a sign you're in an area particularly hard hit by World War II air raids.

The Inquisitor's Palace

MAP P.48, POCKET MAP G9
Main Gate St, Birgu ⓦ heritagemalta.mt.
Charge.

Built as law courts in the thirteenth century, this large Baroque building became the seat for Malta's **Inquisition** between 1574 (when the Knights departed Birgu) and 1798 (when the French arrived), and later served as a military hospital for the British. Your visit begins on the bottom floor – the oldest part of the building, virtually untouched through the ages – with a short film on the Inquisition, before continuing through a compact central courtyard (with its beautiful ribbed cross-vaults) to the palace's kitchens. Ascend a **grand staircase**, designed by Romano Carapecchia, one of the most important Baroque

artists working in early medieval Malta, to the *piano nobile,* the public domain of the Inquisitor. Here, 3D models and projections describe the building's architectural history. On the top floor you'll encounter "authentic artefacts confiscated as proof of misconduct" (primarily banned books, which were burnt in front of crowds in Birgu's main square). Next, descend to the austere **Tribunal Room**, entered through a half-sized door intended to force even the most unwilling of prisoners to bow to the Inquisitor's authority. In 1607, Baroque artist Caravaggio (see page 34) was a witness in a case of bigamy here. Round things off with a walk through the palace's **prisons**, where the anguished graffiti of internees is still visible on the walls.

St Lawrence Church

MAP P.48, POCKET MAP G9
St Lawrence St, Birgu.

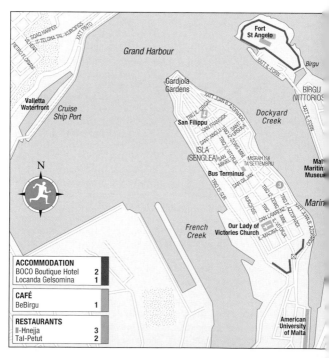

ACCOMMODATION	
BOCO Boutique Hotel	2
Locanda Gelsomina	1

CAFÉ	
BeBirgu	1

RESTAURANTS	
Il-Hnejja	3
Tal-Petut	2

Visiting the Three Cities

Getting to the Three Cities is straightforward, but it's best to plan ahead: this series of peninsulas look closer than they are, and most routes pass through a series of bays and villages that lengthen your journey. **Buses** #2 & 3 from Valletta pass through Bormla to Birgu, with #3 continuing to Kalkara and Fort Rinella. Bus #4 from Valletta skirts Bormla and terminates at Birgu. A faster and more pleasant way to arrive is by **ferry** from Valletta, departing from Barriera Wharf (descend the lift to the ferry landing from Upper Barrakka Gardens). Ferries depart every 30min. Alternately, you can hire a **traditional wooden boat**, known as a *dgħajsa,* to take you across the harbour (specify if you wish to embark at Isla or Birgu when you board). Fares include transport and a 30min tour of the Grand Harbour. *Dgħajsas* queue for passengers next to the ferry. If you plan to return to Valletta by boat, the ferry is a more reliable option; *dgħajsas* are independently operated with fluctuating schedules and some require a minimum number of passengers to depart.

St Lawrence Church sits evocatively atop a high parapet at the town's marina entrance, making it a key part of the village's skyline. The original building was one of Malta's earliest medieval parish churches, and it later served as the Knights' conventual church

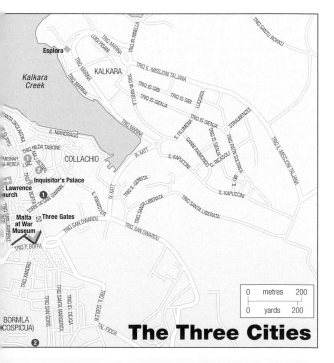

The Three Cities

Malta Maritime Museum

galleys. Paintings of famous sea battles, cannons, anchors and salvaged pieces of ships from the past five centuries complete the collection. The largest hall is dedicated to the legacy of the Royal Navy in Malta, from its wartime role to the more recent history of the drydocks at Isla, and includes a charming reconstruction of a sailor's pub.

Fort St Angelo

MAP P.48, POCKET MAP F8
Birgu Waterfront ⓦ heritagemalta.com.
Charge.

Fort St Angelo sits at the tip of Birgu's peninsula, dominating the Grand Harbour with its dramatic vertical layers of limestone fortifications. No other fortress has been as critical in shaping the country's history and, now restored, it is at long last open to the public.

The history of the fortress dates back to at least the thirteenth century, when the Sicilian overlords kept a small *Castrum Maris* (castle by the sea) here. In 1530, the Knights of the Order of St John took the fort as their headquarters, extensively remodelling it and introducing the bastioned system of defence to Malta. The fort would play a major role in the three-month Great Siege of 1565 as the provisions depot and command centre of Grand Master Jean Parisot de Valette, who led a force of some 600 Knights and a few thousand men-at-arms against more than 40,000 Turks – with Fort St Angelo's cannons bombarding the invading forces throughout the Siege, it became a symbol of perseverance and survival against the odds. Over the next three centuries, the fort's defences were continuously strengthened. During World War II, the fortress suffered 69 direct bomb hits owing to its role as the British headquarters, which it relinquished when the Lascaris War Rooms (see page 27) were built. After the war, the fortress remained the shore base

between 1530 and 1571 until the Knights were transferred to Valletta. The present structure dates from 1681 and was the first of a spate of triumphal churches designed by master Maltese architect Lorenzo Gafa, who shunned the fad for ornate Baroque during his time, achieving a grand presence with architectural setting and composition. The highlight of its interior is the altarpiece by Italian Baroque artist Mattia Preti – a tense depiction of the martyrdom of St Lawrence and Preti's largest ever painting. During World War II, the church suffered multiple bombings, one of which destroyed its dome, later rebuilt in the early 1950s.

Malta Maritime Museum

MAP P.48, POCKET MAP G9
Birgu Waterfront ⓦ heritagemalta.mt.
Charge.

Situated in the British-built former naval bakery, the **Maritime Museum** holds an interesting collection pertaining to Malta's illustrious seafaring history. Exhibits consist mainly of models of ships, from the diminutive *dghajsa* to exuberant Knightly

of the British navy until March 31, 1979, when the last British sailors left Malta.

Visits begin by climbing ever deeper and higher into the fortress to arrive at the **Ferramolino Cavalier**, located at the fort's southwestern point. Here, three lofty vaults have been transformed into immersive audiovisual experiences (the fort's only formal museum spaces), each describing a different aspect of local history, from the country's millennia of foreign occupation to Fort St Angelo's history and cultural symbolism. After visiting the vaults, you are free to wander about the fortress complex to take in its vast size; climb to the very top for 360-degree views, with the northeastern tip looking out towards Valletta. Access to the Upper Fort is restricted to a limited number of tours and pre-booking is required. Here you'll find **The Magisterial Palace, St Anne's Chapel**, and a private residence for the only resident Knight on the island.

Bormla

MAP P.48, POCKET MAP F9

Bormla (Cospicua), which can trace its origins to megalithic times, has been used by Phoenicians, Romans, Normans and the Knights of St John as a refuge for ships and a hub for commerce and defence. Today, Bormla's motto, *Ingens Amplectitur Agger* (embraced by bastions), perfectly describes the village, which connects the peninsulas of Birgu and Isla (it's often difficult to tell where one village ends and the others begin). A walk along Birgu's pretty harbourfront promenade will bring you to Bormla's Dock 1, which served as the Royal Navy Dockyard and was an important supply base during World War I and World War II. Today, the dockyard is home to the **American University of Malta**.

Bormla's alternate name, *Cospicua*, is a derivative of "conspicuous," so-called because the town lay outside Birgu's fortifications

during the Great Siege and was razed to the ground. It was rebuilt and protected by an arc of fortifications (**The Margarita Lines**) that encircle the Three Cities. Eventually, advances in military technology and the modernization of the Ottoman striking armada rendered the Margarita Lines ineffective – an enemy situated on the hillocks outside the wall could lob cannon shells into the Three Cities – and this led to the conception of a second-tier wall beyond the Margarita Lines, called the **Cottonera Lines**. Wholly intact to this day, the Cottonera Lines envelop the Three Cities with a heavy semi-circular wall studded with eight triangular bastions (to facilitate a 360-degree sweep of fire) and two demi-bastions where they connect with the fortifications of Isla and Birgu.

Isla

MAP P.48, POCKET MAP F9

Isla (Senglea) was founded by Knights in the 1550s and takes its name from Claude de la Sengle, Grand Master at the time. Isla was severely damaged in the Great Siege of 1565, and some four hundred years later it was almost completely razed again during World War II. With a population of almost 3000 living in an area of just 0.2 square kilometres, Isla is one of the most densely populated cities in the world, but harbour views on all sides keep it from feeling congested. The best way to access the city is from the promenade opposite Birgu. Climbing any staircase from here will take you to the town's main road, Triq Il-Vitorja, which stretches almost all the way to the tip of the peninsula and offers splendid views of the **marina** to the east (a recently gentrified part of the city) and a **dockyard** to the west (where oil rigs often come in for repairs). The town's parish church, **Our Ladies of Victories**, is in the main square,

Misraħ Papa Benedittu XV (free). It was completely rebuilt after being obliterated during World War II to clear the way for German aircraft to dive-bomb Malta's dockyards.

The highlight of any visit to Isla is the city's oldest area, which survived the war and lies at the tip of Isla's peninsula. The charming alleys and townhouses here are reminiscent of those in Birgu and Valletta yet, located high above and surrounded by the sea on all sides, the neighbourhood offers a distinct flavour. Reaching the end of the peninsula brings you to **Gardjola Gardens** (free), which is not really a garden but a monument to the *gardjola* (sentry post) that overlooks the harbour here. Take note of the structure's sculpted eye and ear, meant as a warning that the Knights had eyes and ears everywhere. The garden offers excellent views of the Grand Harbour and Fort St Angelo. On Isla's promenade, stop at *il-Ħnejja* (see page 53) for lunch, admiring traditional wooden fishing boats moored next to impressive yachts in the waters separating Isla and Birgu. On late summer afternoons local children gather here to swim and elderly men to fish.

Fort Rinella

MAP P.48, POCKET MAP H7
Saint Rokku St, Kalkara ⓦ fortrinella.com.
Charge, including tour and short film.
Bus #3 from Valletta. Free shuttle service (book online).

Particularly for history enthusiasts, **Fort Rinella** is well worth straying off the beaten path for. Lying north of the Three Cities in the town of Kalkara, Fort Rinella was erected by the British in the 1870s specifically to operate the Armstrong 100-ton gun. The largest cannon ever made, it was designed so that its shells could pierce the steel plates of ships as far as three miles away, thereby protecting the sea routes leading to the Grand Harbour. It was fired just forty times, the last in 1905, but

it's unclear from historical records whether it ever actually hit anything it was aimed at. The fort itself is a one of Malta's few examples of Victorian military architecture, and has been sensitively restored by local volunteer group Wirt Artna. Period furnishings and decor have been re-created, and you can study the intricate machinery that operated the Armstrong – the gun is so heavy that it needed a mini coal-fired power station to turn its barrel for aiming. Superb hourly demonstrations and historic re-enactment displays evoke life here during its heyday. The main guided tour (2pm) includes interactive military drills, the firing of period artillery and a cavalry show with charming volunteers and lovingly tended rescue horses.

Esplora

MAP P.48, POCKET MAP G8
Marina St, Kalkara ⓦ esplora.org.mt.
Charge (additional charge for planetarium).

Malta's national interactive science centre, **Esplora**, is located at **Villa Bighi**, built in 1675 as a retirement villa by Fra Giovanni Bichi, an Italian Knight, and occupied for the next century by his descendants and a colourful variety of noblemen. In 1801 the site was identified by Dr J. Stripe, Lord Admiral Nelson's chief physician, as a prime location for a new naval hospital, which fell into disuse after the Royal Navy's departure in 1979. In 2016, Villa Bighi was transformed into Esplora, a splendid, sprawling science centre with plenty besides beautiful views and architecture to occupy the young and young-at-heart. A planetarium suspended within the ruins of a World War II-bombed building is a notable architectural element, but the kitschy films screened here will only appeal to very young visitors. A programme of interactive demonstrations for children changes daily and the on-site café offers standard fare.

Café

BeBirgu

MAP P.48, POCKET MAP G9
Misraħ ir-Rebħa 11, Birgu
ⓦ facebook.com/Bebirgu.

Located in the St Lawrence Band Club, this relaxed café and bar's unique, surprisingly palatial setting makes up for its average cuisine. Its chefs are Belgian and German, so mussels and great German beer are always on the (affordable) menu. €

Restaurants

Il-Ħnejja

MAP P.48, POCKET MAP F9
14 Xatt Juan B Azzopardo, Isla
ⓦ facebook.com/Hnejja.

Eat like a local at *il-Ħnejja*, an excellent little family-run place on Isla's promenade with plenty of seaside seating. Undoubtedly the best restaurant in Isla, *Il-Ħnejja*

Fort Rinella from St Elmo

offers delicious fresh seafood and pasta, including lobster ravioli and sea-urchin spaghetti. If you can't make up your mind on what to order, the restaurant will serve a platter of various pastas. €€

Tal-Petut

MAP P.48, POCKET MAP G9
20 Pacifiku Scicluna St, Birgu
ⓦ talpetut.com.

Unmissable *Tal-Petut* offers a "private dining" experience which, owing to the warm hospitality of cook and host, Donald Caligari Conti (who never forgets a name or face), manages to be intimate, elegant and relaxed at once. There's no menu here, just a multi-course experience of the best Maltese food that takes "made from scratch" to new heights (Donald even sun-dries the tomatoes), employing fresh, seasonal ingredients according to the restaurant's motto: "Mother Nature is the chef; we are the cooks". €€€

Sliema and St Julian's

Malta's cosmopolitan hub sprawls along its rocky coastline for some 5km, from the harbourfront villages of Gżira and Sliema to the nightlife hubs of St Julian's and Paċeville. These two relatively young towns emerged as the island's entertainment centres in the 1980s; in the 1990s a string of luxury hotels and condominiums pushed the area further upscale. Modern facilities pull in the tourists, and despite having no historic attractions, good transport connections make the area a convenient base, while remaining close to the nightlife scene.

Sliema and St Julian's

MAP P.56, POCKET MAP A2–E5

Once quiet fishing hamlets, Sliema and St Julian's became urban hubs in the nineteenth century when Valletta residents built colourful Victorian summer homes and the British installed coastal fortifications here. Sadly, both are disappearing to make way for modern skyscrapers, but this juxtaposition of old and new is part of this area's unique character.

Promenade in Sliema

Sliema and St Julian's are synonymous with the sea and shopping. A stroll along the pretty seaside **promenade** they share is an essential part of any visit. Begin at Gżira's Manoel Island (see page 55) and you can follow the coastline for 5km to St Julian's Spinola Bay. The stretch that faces Valletta's skyline is The Strand, Malta's main shopping district. This leads to Tigne Point, a luxury residential complex and shopping mall. Tigne Point connects on to Tower Road, the main stretch of the promenade facing a wide rocky shoreline beloved by tourists, teenage English-language students and local families for swimming and seaside BBQs. During the summer, the majority of this shoreline is a protected swimming zone (if you prefer a dip in a pool, visit a nearby lido; see page 58). In the winter, rough seas make swimming here inadvisable, but sea views from the promenade are still captivating (and the star attraction of a staggering number of restaurants and bars).

There are a few historic points of interest too. During the 1565 Great Siege, Ottoman Admiral Dragut Rais stationed his troops at Sliema's Tigne Point, where he was killed in a bombardment. In 1789, St Julian's entered the history books as the first

Traditional colourful Maltese balconies in Sliema

town to be conquered in the French occupation (Spinola Bay is believed to be where Napoleon landed).

Gżira

MAP P.56, POCKET MAP B5

Gżira, Sliema's less glamorous, less expensive sister village, is the starting point for the promenade (see page 54) that extends to St Julian's. The village enjoys lovely views of Valletta's skyline, although a busy marina means there are no swimming zones here. Gżira is named after nearby **Manoel Island** (*gżira* means "island"), where visitors can cross a short bridge to find a duck sanctuary and, in the

Visiting Sliema and St Julian's

Sliema and St Julian's are well served by **buses** (Ⓦpublictransport.com.mt), with frequent stops along the promenade (see page 54) and a few routes through the villages' centres. The main bus terminal is located in Sliema, where a ferry connects Sliema to Valletta at the aptly named Sliema Ferries area. Hop-on hop-off tour buses also stop throughout Sliema and St Julian's, some calling at specific hotels and resorts. Sliema and St Julian's have Malta's highest concentration of **Next Bikes** (rental bicycles; see page 139).

It's difficult to find a **parking spot** in Sliema and St Julian's congested streets. Your best bet is the multi-storey car park on High Street in Sliema's shopping zone; in St Julian's try Spinola Park (Mikiel Ang Borg Street, Spinola Bay), Eden Park (St Augustine Street, Paceville) or the more expensive car park at Portomaso (Portomaso Road). For **taxis**, try St Julian's-headquartered eCabs (Ⓣ2138 3838, Ⓦecabs.com.mt), Yellow Cabs (Ⓣ2298 2298, Ⓦyellow.com.mt) or Greenr (Ⓣ2738 3838, Ⓦfacebook.com/GreenrCabsMalta), all of which operate 24/7.

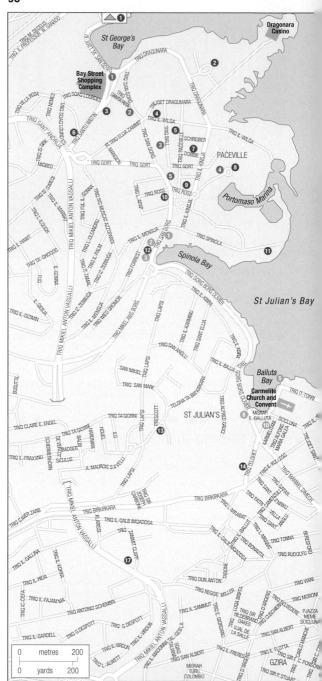

Dragonara
Casino

St George's
Bay

Bay Street
Shopping
Complex

TRIQ DRAGUNARA

TRIQ SANTA RITA

SANTA RITA

TRIQ SQAQ LOURDES

TRIQ VILLA ROSA

TRIQ NEMSIS

TRIQ SAN ANDRIJA

TRIQ IS-SIRK

TRIQ M. DE DELS

TRIQ IL-PROFESSUR W. GANADO

JX-XATT TA' SAN GORG

TRIQ DRAGUNARA

TRIQ DRAGUNARA

TRIQ SAN GORG

TREJQET DRAGUNARA

TRIQ IL-WILGA

TRIQ IL-WILGA

SCHREIBER

DOBBIE

PACEVILLE

TRIQ ELLUL ZAMMIT

TRIQ SAN GORG

TRIQ SAN GORG

TRIQ IL-KNISJA

TRIQ IL MANSION

TRIQ GORT

TRIQ GORT

TRIQ GORT

TRIQ GORT

Portomaso Marina

TRIQ SANTU WISTIN

MIGBED

TRIQ FUL IL-GONNA

TRIQ IL-OLEANDRI

TRIQ MIKIEL ANTON VASSALLI

TRIQ IL-PALM

TRIQ ROSS

TRIQ ROSS

TRIQ LAPP

TRIQ IL-MENSIJA

TRIQ SAN GORG

TRIQ SPINOLA

Spinola Bay

St Julian's Bay

TRIQ IL-HAWT

TRIQ IL-CLIGH

TRIQ S'ANDRIJA MARSALL

TRIQ IL-MARONI

TRIQ IL-OLEANDRI

TRIQ IL-GIZIRA

TRIQ TA' GHODOD

FLUS

FRANCO 2F

TRIQ FORREST

TRIQ WIED GHOMOR

TRIQ IL-GIZIMIN

TRIQ MIKIEL ANG BORG

TRIQ GORG BORG OLIVER

TRIQ IL-KSBRA

TRIQ IL-KARRIMUL

TRIQ SANT ELIA

TRIQ SAN ANGLU

TRIQ IL-BAJJA

TRIQ GORG BORG OLIVER

TRIQ IL-KSBRA

BUSITTIL

Balluta
Bay

Carmelite
Church and
Convent

SAN MIKIEL

TRIQ SAN MARK

TELGHA TA' BIRBARBARA

SAN MIKIEL

ST JULIAN'S

MISRAH
IL-BALLUTA

KARMELITANI

TRIQ ALFRED OVUCI

TRIQ ALFONS MARIA GALEA

TRIQ IT-TORRI

TREJQET SANT

SCICLUNA

TRIQ CLAIRE E. ENGEL

TRIQ TA' GIORNI

TRIQ TA' GIORNI

PRESCOTT

RSPQ

TRIQ IL-FRAXXNU

SCHEMBRI

HOLEG

BADGER

SICULUS

PRESCOTT

TRIQ TELGHET

TRIQ IL-KULLEGG

TRIQ GEFAR

TRIQ SANT PATRI CARMELO ZAMMIT

TRIQ MAWIEL DIMECH

TRIQ IL-MRABAT

TRIQ SANT

TRIQ VELLA ANGLU

A. MAUROIS S.A. VELLI

TRIQ LAPS

TRIQ SIR JOSEPH CASSON

TRIQ MIKIEL ANTON VASSALLI

TRIQ SAVER ZARB

KSBRA

TRIQ BIRKIRKARA

TRIQ BIRKIRKARA

TRIQ IL-QALB IMQADDSA

TRIQ IL-OLEANDRI

TRIQ BONAVITA

TRIQ L-ARBGHT

TRIQ TONNA

TRIQ RUDOLFU

PJAZZA
MEME
SCICLUNA

TRIQ ZAMMIT CLAPP

TRIQ DUN ANTON

TRIQ REGGIE MILLER

TRIQ A. SAMMUT

TRIQ E. GIORDANO

TRIQ ARGENS

TRIQ VIANI

TRIQ MORONI

TRIQ IL-GALLINA

TRIQ IL-NIDA

TRIQ IL-KOKKA

TRIQ IC-CEFA

TRIQ IL-FAJAM'MA

TRIQ IL-GARDELL

TRIQ G. DESPOTT

TRIQ ANTONIO SCHEMBRI

TRIQ G. DESPOTT

TRIQ IL-VRDUN

TRIQ IL-VRDUN

TRIQ MIKIEL ANTON VASSALLI

TRIQ IL-MADONNA TAL-GEBLA

OVUS

TRIQ SAN ALBERT

MISRAH
TURU
COLOMBO

TRIQ L-ALWETT

TRIQ SAN P. STUART

TRIQ SIR F.C. PONSONBY

TRIQ IL-FRERES

TRIQ IL-FLOTTA

TRIQ GORG MANGHE

LUCA BRIFFA

TRIQ SIR HILDEBRAND OAKES

VJAL DE
LA SALLE

TRIQ SAN ALBERT

PJAZZA
FEDERIGO

GZIRA

0   metres   200

0   yards   200

Sliema and St Julian's

ACCOMMODATION	
115 The Strand Suites	19
Barceló Fortina	20
Boho Hostel	17
Cavalieri Art Hotel	11
Corinthia Hotel St George's Bay	1
The District Hotel	6
The George	5
Hilton	8
Hostel Malti	13
Hotel Juliani	12
Hotel Valentina	7
IKYK	4
Inhawi Boutique Hostel	14
InterContinental Malta	3
Marco Polo Hostel	10
Onyx Hotel	9
The Palace	16
Pebbles Boutique Aparthotel	18
The Victoria Hotel	15
Westin	2

SHOPS	
Christine X Art Gallery	4
RIOT Boutique	3
Soap Café	1
Souvenirs That Don't Suck	2

CAFÉS	
Café Juliani	2
Finca Velez	6
il-Gabbana	4
Word of Mouth	7

RESTAURANTS	
Ali Baba	13
L'Antica Pizzerria Da Michele	10
Barracuda Restaurant	5
Café Cuba	1
Corner Crave	11
Fernandō Gastrotheque	12
Kebab Ji	9
U Bistrot	8
Zest	3

BARS AND CLUBS	
Black Gold	8
Club Havana	2
Cork's	5
Hammett's Gastro Bar	7
Hole in the Wall	6
Hugo's Terrace	1
The Thirsty Barber	3
Twenty Two	4

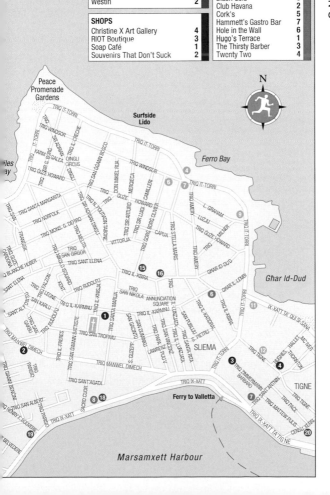

Lidos

If you prefer pools to the sea, visit one of Sliema or St Julian's many freshwater **lidos**, typically open from 9am–7pm and charging a modest entry fee; many hotels and resorts in Sliema and St Julian's also offer day memberships to their pools. Popular establishments include Neptune's (Spinola Bay; ⓦ neptuneswpsc. com), 1926 La Plage (Sliema; ⓦ 1926lesoleil.com) and MedAsia Playa (Sliema; ⓦ medasiaplaya.com), *Corinthia Hotel St George's Bay* (ⓦ corinthia.com; see page 130), the *Radisson Blu* (ⓦ radissonblu. com) and the *Hilton* (ⓦ hilton.com; see page 130) – a great option for travellers staying at B&Bs or apartments.

summer months, a small outdoor fair. The island is dominated by **Fort Manoel**, a beautiful eighteenth-century fortification enclosing a magnificent parade ground and arcade, which is not currently open to visitors – public pressure may see this change in the coming years.

Balluta Bay

MAP P.56, POCKET MAP B3

Sliema slides imperceptibly into St Julian's at **Balluta Bay**, with its busy seaside promenade and

small triangular *pjazza*. Peppered with Judas trees, benches and a few cafés, the square is a nice place for an afternoon drink. Its eastern flank is dominated by the monumental Balluta Buildings, a fantastic 1920s Art Nouveau apartment block whose arches, intricate angel motifs and terraced profile provide an ornate contrast to the otherwise uniform high-rises fringing the bay. Though shallow and sometimes silty, the bay itself is a swimming zone and home to the lido Neptune's (see box).

Carmelite Church, Balluta Bay

Spinola Bay

Spinola Bay

MAP P.56, POCKET MAP A2–B2

Home to legions of restaurants, cafés, bars and hotels, compact, kidney-shaped **Spinola Bay** is always bustling with people strolling along the promenade and watching the fishermen mending nets in front of their boathouses. The bay itself remains home to a dwindling number of moored-up *luzzu*, painted in vibrant colours, decorated with Baroque designs and sporting the much-photographed "Eyes of Osiris" on their bows to lead to good fishing grounds. Many of Spinola Bay's restaurants have terraces overlooking the sea, making it a lovely spot to have dinner, with the lights shimmering romantically and the *LOVE* monument (designed by Richard England) reflecting in the bay's still water.

Paċeville

MAP P.56, POCKET MAP B2

Paċeville is Malta's prime nightlife district, with dozens of bars, clubs and pubs rubbing shoulders at ground level, and high-rise resort-style apartment blocks towering overhead. Deserted by day, Paċeville picks up at night, when thousands of young people descend on the quarter (peak hours are between 11pm and 3am). It's a boisterous, cheap, cheerful and generally amicable scene, with loud music blaring from the open-fronted bars and people spilling onto the pavements. You'll find a more mature crowd at the bars in Sliema or Valletta. If clubbing isn't your scene, Paċeville also offers a small sandy beach (St George's Bay), the Bay Street shopping mall, the seventeen-screen Eden Cinemas and the Eden Bowling Alley.

Shops

Christine X Art Gallery

MAP P.56, POCKET MAP D4

17 Triq Tigne, Sliema Ⓦ christinexart.com.
A small but excellent art gallery exclusively stocking local works, from Maltese landscapes to figurative pieces.

RIOT Boutique

MAP P.56, POCKET MAP D4

Floor 1, Plaza Shopping Centre, Sliema Ⓦ riotboutique.com
This popular shop, run by a youthful team, is one of the best places to pick up street, surf and skate wear, as the only stockist in Malta of brands like Quicksilver and DC Shoes.

Soap Café

MAP P.56, POCKET MAP C4

46 Triq Santa Marija, Sliema Ⓦ soapcafemalta.com.
As its name suggests, Soap Café is a boutique specializing in handmade soaps, lotions, balms and scrubs made from local ingredients like olive oil, goat's milk and purees of local prickly pears and pumpkins. Airline-friendly sizes of most products are available.

Souvenirs That Don't Suck

MAP P.56, POCKET MAP C4

108 Triq Manwel Dimech, Sliema Ⓦ souvenirsthatdontsuck.mt.
That rare thing: a hip souvenir shop. Look for hoodies with the ubiquitous local phrase, "Mela", a word completely unique to the Maltese language, used to mean anything from "so" or "yes" to an expression of surprise.

Cafés

Café Juliani

MAP P.56, POCKET MAP B3

25 St George's Rd, St Julian's Ⓦ cafejuliani.com.
Calm, relaxing café inside the *Hotel Juliani*, overlooking Spinola Bay. Breakfast options include vast Continental sharing platters, Greek yogurt bowls and artichoke frittata, while the lunch and dinner menus include rich curries and ocean-fresh sushi. €€

Christine X Art Gallery

Finca Velez

MAP P.56, POCKET MAP D4
19 Triq Windsor, Sliema ⓦ fincavelez.com.
The Colombian connection is
strong in this colourfully-painted,
plant-strewn café, with beans
roasted in Manizales, in the so-
called Coffee Triangle. Alongside
the great coffee is a menu of lovely
and good-value cakes, salads and
sandwiches. €€

il-Gabbana

MAP P.56, POCKET MAP D3
Triq it-Torri, Sliema ⓦ ilgabbana.com.
Essentially an upscale kiosk,
il-Gabbana offers lovely sea views
and a large outdoor terrace.
Salads, pasta, pizza and burgers
are average but for a perfect light
bite, the *focaccia semplice* is highly
recommended. €€

Word of Mouth

MAP P.56, POCKET MAP D3
30/39 Luzio Junction, Stella Maris Street,
Sliema ⓦ wom.com.mt.
This popular, colourful spot has
quickly established itself as one
of the best places on the island
for brunch, with a wide range of
offerings no matter how hungry
you are – açai bowls, Nutella
pancakes, and healthy salads all the
way up to rib-eye steaks and fish
and chips. €€

Restaurants

Ali Baba

MAP P.56, POCKET MAP B5
9 Triq Ponsomby, Gżira
ⓦ alibaba.hanyharb.com.
Malta's first Lebanese restaurant
was opened more than 25 years ago
and they still make everything by
hand, from the pitta bread to each
and every mouthwatering mezze
– ordering a selection to share is
highly recommended. €€

L'Antica Pizzerria Da Michele

MAP P.56, POCKET MAP B3

10 Balluta Steps, Balluta Bay, St Julian's
ⓦ damichelemalta.com.
Famous as the home of "Malta's
biggest pizza", *Da Michele's* pies are
indeed monstrous in size but are
also truly delicious, surprisingly
light yet packed full of authentic
Neapolitan flavour. There is much
more to the menu besides pies and
pizza, from swordfish steaks to
beef cutlet, ravioli, and many other
pasta offerings. €€

Barracuda Restaurant

MAP P.56, POCKET MAP B3
194 Main Street, St Julian's
ⓦ facebook.com/BarracudaRestaurant.
The *Barracuda Restaurant* of
local and international renown
is housed in a lovingly restored
eighteenth-century villa, located
just over the water's edge and
overlooking the spectacular view
of Balluta and Spinola bay. A
combination of excellent service
and delicious a la carte specialities
will make the evening memorable.
€€€

Café Cuba

MAP P.56, POCKET MAP A2
159 Triq San Ġorġ, Spinola Bay, St Julian's
ⓦ cafecuba.com.mt.
Its name suggests otherwise, but
Café Cuba's focus is Mediterranean
food, including excellent wood-
fired pizzas and focaccia made
with ingredients imported from
Italy. Of its two locations in Sliema
and St Julian's, the latter offers the
loveliest atmosphere, with a large
terrace overlooking pretty Spinola
Bay. €€

Corner Crave

MAP P.56, POCKET MAP D4
8 Qui-Si-Sana, Sliema
ⓦ facebook.com/CornerCraveCafeBistro.
Comfort food is the order of the
day at this buzzing joint by the
beach, popular with hungover
night owls. The burgers are the
headline act, but there's much
more besides, from salmon pasta to
pizzas and bone-in steaks. €€

Fernandō Gastrotheque

MAP P.56, POCKET MAP B3
195 Triq Ġorġ Borg Olivier, St Julian's
Ⓦ fernando.com.mt.

Expect some of the very finest food in Malta at this unpretentious Michelin-starred restaurant, which lets its menu do the talking. Smoked eel with hispi cabbage, Maltese wild fish with caper butter, and Araguani chocolate ganache with Armagnac prunes are a few sample dishes, all simple, beautifully done, and maximizing local produce. €€€

Kebab Ji

MAP P.56, POCKET MAP D3
124 Triq it-Torri, Sliema
Ⓦ facebook.com/kebabji.grill

This casual Lebanese offers reliably good and affordable salads, kebabs, falafel, pita and *shawarma* prepared fresh to order. Busy at all hours with takeaway custom, there are also a few tables for eating in. €

U Bistrot

MAP P.56, POCKET MAP B3
195 Triq Ġorġ Borg Olivier, St Julian's
Ⓦ ubistrot.com.

A popular bistro overlooking Balluta Bay serving a small but

Fernandō Gastrotheque

excellent healthy, seasonal menu (including low-calorie options). Before noon, try the reliable full English and delicious pancakes and eggs Benedict. For lunch and dinner, expect salads, pastas, homemade burgers and grilled fish. €€

Zest

MAP P.56, POCKET MAP A2
25 Triq San Ġorġ, St Julian's
Ⓦ zestflavours.com.

Zest introduced the Asian Fusion concept to Malta in 2002 and has been a favourite amongst locals since. House specialities include Indonesian beef rendang and top-notch sushi. During the summer, tables on the restaurant's small terrace offer lovely sunset views. €€

Bars and clubs

Black Gold

MAP P.56, POCKET MAP C5
Triq Ix-Xatt, Gżira
Ⓦ facebook.com/BlackGoldMalta.

This casual watering hole is more of a café-style joint during the day. In the evenings it morphs into a more boisterous and beer-fuelled bar, especially on weekends when it's likely to stay open until early morning. The music is a mix of rock and other genres, and sports matches are regularly shown.

Club Havana

MAP P.56, POCKET MAP A1
86 Triq San Ġorġ, Paċeville ☎ 2137 4500.

A popular club that is usually full (and sweaty) at weekends with a young crowd. The ground floor specializes in hip-hop, while the upper level leans more towards r'n'b and soul.

Cork's

MAP P.56, POCKET MAP A2
58 Triq San Ġorġ, Paċeville ☎ 2135 3660.

Think good Guinness, live Irish music, a raucous yet friendly atmosphere, and a predominantly

Hole in the Wall

Irish and British clientele. Also authentic is the drunkenness on show at the pub's karaoke nights (Thurs–Sun). Major sports matches regularly screened.

Hammett's Gastro Bar

MAP P.56, POCKET MAP D4
33/34 Tigne Seafront, Sliema
Ⓦ hammettsgastrobar.com.
This gastro bar, located in Sliema's busy shopping district, is at its busiest for aperitivo, when stylish shoppers take residence to catch up on gossip over wine, cocktails and tapas.

Hole in the Wall

MAP P.56, POCKET MAP D4
31 Triq Kbira, Sliema
Ⓦ holeinthewall.com.mt.
Tucked on a quiet side street just off of Sliema's main shopping area, this ninety-year-old pub has some of the most affordable prices in this (typically overpriced) village. Despite its diminutive size, it frequently hosts top-notch gigs with Malta's best and up-and-coming acts.

Hugo's Terrace

MAP P.56, POCKET MAP A1
St George's Bay, Paceville
Ⓦ hugosterrace.com.

A comfortable lounge popular with a more mature crowd of locals and expats that offers a dance floor (with DJs mixing lounge and house music) within sight of St George's Bay Beach.

The Thirsty Barber

MAP P.56, POCKET MAP A1
Triq Ball, St Julian's
Ⓦ thethirstybarber.com.
A hip, speakeasy-themed cocktail bar with a "hidden" entrance through a red telephone box. The upmarket menu revives typical Prohibition recipes, such as the Paper Plane (created in London's Ritz Hotel in the 1920s), prepared with Brazilian lime juice and Amaro Nonino.

Twenty Two

MAP P.56, POCKET MAP B2
Level 22, Portomaso Business Tower, St Julian's ☏ 2310 2222.
Twenty Two is all about superlatives: it's the country's poshest, most exclusive club (with prices to match), with the best views from atop Malta's tallest building. Expect a mature, affluent, smartly dressed crowd enjoying chill-out tunes. There's usually a nominal cover charge and reservations are essential on weekends.

Mdina and Rabat

With everything from Malta's ancient capital, frozen in time, to rolling green valleys and the rugged heights of the nearby coast, the island's western region has a distinct feel and allure, and should be a part of any itinerary. Start with Mdina, a majestic pedestrianized village enclosed by early medieval fortifications, before hitting its neighbour, Rabat, which has an eclectic mix of underground sights from the same period. To the west lie Malta's largest woodland and the dramatic Dingli Cliffs, which tumble down to Fomm Ir-Riħ, a wildly beautiful bay.

Mdina

MAP P.66, POCKET MAP D14

With views of most of the country from atop its golden ring of fortifications, tiny, achingly beautiful **Mdina** is one of Malta's major highlights. One of the island's earliest urban settlements, it also served as the capital until Valletta took over in 1571. First established by the Phoenicians and later taken over by the Romans

An old street in Mdina

(who named it Melite), ancient Mdina used to be up to three times its current size. Legend has it that when Paul the Apostle was shipwrecked in Malta in 60 CE, he was greeted by Publius, the governor of Melite, who became the first Bishop of Malta. Few remains survive from the Roman period, with the most significant at Domus Romana (see page 69). As the Western Roman Empire fell and Melite slid into the early medieval era, a dry moat was built, reducing the city to its present size.

The village's mazes of narrow, twisting alleys were designed to disorient invading forces and today maintain their distinctly medieval feel. With tumbling pink bougainvillea and pretty archways, photo opportunities here abound. The Knights could not resist adding a Baroque flair to the city in the eighteenth century with the addition of the Main Gate and Magisterial Palace (see page 65), both picturesque in their own right. Virtually car-free and with just three hundred inhabitants (including cloistered nuns and several noble families), by night Mdina feels frozen in time under a cloak of silence. By day, it's a regular haunt for tour groups but, nonetheless, an unforgettable setting.

Mdina's Main Gate

The Main Gate and Pjazza San Publiju

MAP P.66

Mdina's Main Gate was a Baroque contribution by the Knights built in 1724. It formed part of a restoration programme overseen by Grand Master Manoel de Vilhena, which saw the gate shifted east (you can still see the outline of its medieval predecessor to one side) so that it would lead directly to the planned Magisterial Palace. Below the gate is a dry moat, recently turned into a

A Mdina walking tour

If you only have an hour or so here, forget street names and let your feet and eyes guide you through Mdina's series of small *pjazzas* and winding alleys (the village is so small it's impossible to remain lost for long). Don't overlook the lovely coats of arms and elaborate bronze door knockers adorning many facades.

If you prefer a more focused walking tour, follow Mdina's main street – Triq Villegaignon – which connects Mdina end-to-end. The village's most exuberant palaces and several cloisters find their address here, and the street also leads to the main square, Pjazza San Pawl, where you can't miss the huge Cathedral of St Paul. Further on is Palazzo Santo Sofia, one of Mdina's oldest buildings, recognisable from the street-tunnel that cuts through its ground floor, and a fine example of Siculo-Norman architecture (a hybrid of Norman and Sicilian styles found only in Malta). At the end of Triq Villegaignon, Bastion Square is backed by elegant houses and dotted with ficus trees; from here – 140m above sea level – you can admire the expansive view of nearly half the country from one of Malta's highest points. To the southeast, the skyline of Valletta and St Julian's are easily discernible and, to the northeast, the Mosta Dome (see page 75).

Inside St Paul's Cathedral

pretty public garden that is accessible by descending the stairs below *Il-Veduta* restaurant to the southeast. Mind your step as you enter the Main Gate, which is frequented by horse-drawn carriages called *karrozin* – a rather unnecessary tourist trap in this perfectly compact, pedestrianized town.

Magisterial Palace

MAP P.66
Pjazza Publiju.

Built in 1724, the Magisterial Palace was designed by French architect François de Mondion under the patronage of Grand Master de Vilhena, who spent his summers here away from public life in Valletta. The palace's interior was first pared down when it was converted into a hospital under British rule, and further ruined in 1973 when it was reopened as the Museum of Natural History (Ⓦheritagemalta.mt; charge), with

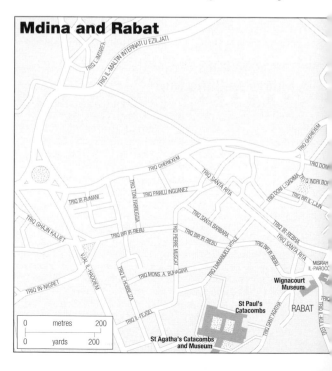

Mdina and Rabat

TRIQ L-IMTARFA
TRIQ IL-MALTIN INTERNATI U EZILJATI
TRIQ GHERIEXEM
TRIQ GHERIEXEM
TRIQ SANTA RITA
TRIQ DON
TRIQ DON L-QADUMA TRIQ Q. INDRI BO?
TRIQ BIR IL-LJUN
TRIQ TON FARRUGIA
TRIQ PAWLU INGUANEZ
TRIQ IR-RUMANI
TRIQ SANTA BARBARA
TRIQ IR-REBHA
TRIQ SANTA RITA
TRIQ GHAJN KAJJET
TRIQ BIR IR-RIEBU
TRIQ BIR IR-RIEBU
TRIQ PJERRE MUSCAT
TRIQ BIR IR-RIEBU
MISRAH IL-PAROCC
VJAL IL-HADDIEM
TRIQ IL-HOBBEJZA
TRIQ MONS. A. BUHAGIAR
TRIQ EMMANUEL VITALE
Wignacourt Museum
TRIQ IN-NIGRET
St Paul's Catacombs
RABAT
TRIQ IL-FEJGEL
TRIQ SANT'AGATHA
TRIQ IL-KBIR
St Agatha's Catacombs and Museum

| 0 | metres | 200 |
| 0 | yards | 200 |

Visiting Mdina and Rabat

Mdina and Rabat are reached on **buses** #51, #52, #53 and #56 from Valletta, #65 from Sliema and #86 from Buġibba. Bus #81 from Valletta passes Mdina and Rabat and continues to Il-Buskett and Dingli Cliffs. There are two public **car parks** between Mdina and Rabat, and both villages are easily (and best) explored on foot.

a worn-out collection that is hardly worth perusing. Do take a look at the palace's elegant facade, though, which survives intact.

St Paul's Cathedral

MAP P.66
Pjazza San Pawl
Ⓦ **metropolitanchapter.com. Charge for the Cathedral and Museum.**

The seat of the Archdiocese of Malta (a function shared with St John's Co-Cathedral; see page 33), **St Paul's Cathedral** majestically dominates the skyline for miles around. Dedicated to

Malta's most venerated saint, it was built to replace an earlier twelfth-century cathedral that collapsed in a major earthquake in 1693 (the 7.4 magnitude quake also devastated Sicily and badly damaged buildings in Valletta and the Three Cities). It was designed by the best-known Maltese architect of the time, Lorenzo Gafa, who, unlike his peers, shunned the ornateness of Baroque. Gafa achieved a grand presence by designing a facade with square proportions, the width equal to the height, a

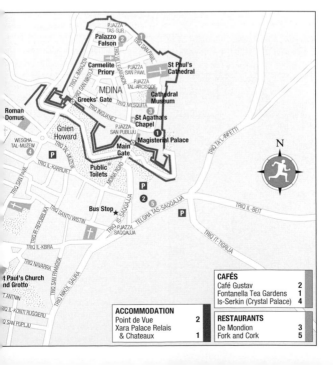

CAFÉS
Café Gustav — 2
Fontanella Tea Gardens — 1
Is-Serkin (Crystal Palace) — 4

ACCOMMODATION
Point de Vue — 2
Xara Palace Relais & Chateaux — 1

RESTAURANTS
De Mondion — 3
Fork and Cork — 5

stylistic technique that is unusual in churches. The two clocks on the facade are a nineteenth-century addition; one shows the hour, the other the calendar.

Mdina's cathedral offers a more restrained interior compared to St John's Co-Cathedral's celebration of Knightly excess. At ground level, six modest side chapels contribute to a sombre atmosphere, and 134 variegated marble tombstones patchwork the floor of the nave, marking the graves of venerated clerics and laymen from noble families. Two large and atmospheric paintings by Mattia Preti in the chancel survive from the original Norman church. Crane your neck higher and you are rewarded with an abundance of ceiling frescoes and gold gilding, beautifully lit by the windows lining the cathedral's uppermost level. The ceiling frescoes depict the life of St Paul, painted by Sicilian brothers and artists Vincenzo, Antonio and

Palazzo Falson

Francesco Manno in the eighteenth century; the frescoes inside the dome are the nineteenth-century work of Giuseppe Gallucci.

Cathedral Museum

MAP P.66
Pjazza tal-Arcisqof Ⓦ metropolitanchapter. com. Same ticket and hours as cathedral.
Across the road from the cathedral (and included in your ticket), the **Cathedral Museum** is a repository for the cathedral's moveable arts accumulated over the centuries. Housed in the former Diocesan Seminary, a Baroque palace built in 1733–40, it is the largest private museum in Malta. An entire room is dedicated to the museum's excellent collection of German Renaissance artist Albrecht Dürer's woodcuts and copper plates, donated to the museum in 1831 by French Count Saverio Marchese (1757–1833). Additional exhibitions of note include an extensive silver and coin collection, ecclesiastical vestments, original manuscripts, ancient reliquaries, an Annunciation altarpiece by French artist Antoine de Favray, and – perhaps the most impressive piece in the museum – a huge fifteenth-century polyptych by Luis Borrassa showing scenes from the life of St Paul.

Palazzo Falson

MAP P.66
Triq il-Villegaignon Ⓦ palazzofalson.com. Charge.
Palazzo Falson is the best surviving example of the style of two-storey Siculo-Norman medieval palace favoured by Sicilian, Spanish and local nobility in Mdina. This fascinating private museum's collection of historical art includes paintings, silver items, furniture, jewellery and rugs. A compact and beautiful library contains more than 4500 books and valuable manuscripts, while on the walls of the Armoury an array of swords, pole arms, pistols and guns are on

The beautiful interior of Carmelite Priory

display. The collection was amassed by Olof Gollcher, who bought the house in 1927 and spent his vast wealth (inherited from his family's shipping line) on filling it with treasures scavenged during his travels. Highlights of the collection include a Robert Robin fob watch with a ten-hour dial that still tells French Revolutionary time (perhaps one of the few that still exist) and several good paintings, including Mattia Preti's *Lucretia Stabbing Herself*, and Edward Lear's take on the idyllic and tranquil coastal landscapes in Malta. An audioguide included with the entry ticket helps explain the displays.

Carmelite Priory

MAP P.66
Triq il-Villegaignon ⓦ carmelitepriory.org. Free; open by appointment.

The seventeenth-century Carmelite Priory in Mdina is the only priory in Malta open to visitors. The highlight of any visit is the Refectory (where friars congregated for communal meals) – no surface is left untouched by pastel frescoes, pink damask, trompe l'oeil paintings and marble. Other rooms

provide a glimpse of friars' daily life. Tours end at the adjoining Carmelite Church, with its spectacular egg-shaped dome and candy-floss pink interior.

Roman Domus

MAP P.66
Wesgħa tal-Mużew, Mdina
ⓦ heritagemalta.mt. Charge.

A repository for most of Malta's small collection of Roman relics, the **Roman Domus** museum is built around the remains of its star attraction, a Roman villa that was unearthed in 1881. It dates from around 50 CE, and is one of twenty-five Roman villas in Malta that are thought to have served as the homesteads of large agricultural estates, probably producing olive oil. The location of this building on the outskirts of Mdina (then Malta's de-facto capital), as well as the life-sized statues discovered within of Emperor Claudius and his mother Antonia, suggest that it belonged to a senior Roman figure. Now only the peristyle, with a splendid mosaic floor depicting the drinking doves of Sosos (a famous and popular motif of

Path to the Roman Domus museum

antiquity, which can also be seen in Pompeii and Rome), survives from the original house. Tours end at the adjoining Muslim cemetery, established in the eleventh century and home to at least 245 burial sites. Artefacts discovered during excavations here are also on display inside the Roman villa, including limestone sarcophagi and tombstones inscribed with beautiful, looping Kufic script.

Rabat

MAP P.66, POCKET MAP D14–15

Five minutes' walk south of Mdina along charming Triq San Pawl brings you to Rabat's town square, to which Mdina's walls stretched until Arab rule (870–1090 CE). The Arabs rebuilt the fortifications on a smaller scale for better defensibility, in effect creating a new suburb (rabat means suburb in Arabic), which eventually grew into a town. The most charming part of Rabat are a series of winding narrow streets (mostly devoid of cars) on the boundary between Mdina and Rabat, well worth

exploring by foot. On March 19 the village celebrates its largest *festa* (dedicated to St Joseph, also a public holiday), during which this area is beautifully decorated in enormous pale blue, white and gold banners and twinkling lights.

St Paul's Catacombs

MAP P.66

Triq Sant Agata, Rabat ◎ heritagemalta.mt. Charge.

Rabat's main sight, **St Paul's Catacombs**, date back to the time when Rabat was part of Mdina and early Christians buried their dead outside the city walls. This dark maze of burial chambers, dug in the fourth and fifth centuries, offers the earliest archaeological evidence of Christianity in Malta. Although small compared to Rome's catacombs, the site offers a good example of Maltese underground architecture, a wholly unique development that was barely influenced by outside traditions.

A visit begins at the excellent visitor centre, which offers a brief introduction to burial traditions and artefacts as well as a short film. Cross the street to enter the underground complex, which first presents two large halls. An interesting feature of the catacombs found here is the Agape table, likely used in funerary rituals where a final meal was shared between living and deceased. From here, raised pathways and atmospheric lighting propel you forward through the labyrinthine passageways. A number of different terraced levels cover an area of over two thousand square metres, and more than a thousand sarcophagi occupying every conceivable space.

St Paul's Church, Wignacourt Museum and Grotto

MAP P.66
Triq ir-Rebha, Rabat
ⓦ wignacourtmuseum.com. Charge.
Rabat's town square is dominated by **St Paul's Church**, which stands on a site where a church is known to have existed since 1372 (though the present Baroque building dates

from 1653). Designed by Francesco Buonamici (who introduced Baroque architecture to Malta), it has an unusually wide, squat facade. For a church with such a lengthy history, the interior is surprisingly bare and bland. The adjoining Wignacourt Museum presents a series of liturgical artefacts and religious paintings.

St Paul's **grotto** is said to have been the hiding place of the saint during his three-month stint in Malta in 60 CE while awaiting his transfer to Rome to stand trial. It's a small, damp and dull place, but its saintly association made this a pilgrimage site during the Knights' time. More recently, Pope Jean Paul II and Pope Benedict have both made a point of praying here during their visits to Malta, but today the site is more popular with tour groups than with pilgrims. Doubling back to the cave's entrance, staircases descend into a labyrinth of third-century Roman catacombs (sadly looted over the centuries and quite devoid of

St Paul's Catacombs

artefacts) and World War II air-raid shelters. The latter boast more than fifty rooms that were hand dug to provide wartime refuge.

St Agatha's Catacombs

MAP P.66
Triq Sant Agata, Rabat
ⓦ stagathamalta.com. Charge.

Located directly opposite St Paul's Catacombs, **St Agatha's** was in use from the Byzantine era (400 CE) through to the seventeenth century as a large burial complex of some four thousand square metres, of which only portions are publicly accessible. Also here is a crypt where St Agatha supposedly hid in 249 CE after she fled Roman persecution in Catania. Access to this atmospheric site is by guided tour only (every 30min, included in entrance fee), which begin at the crypt's two adjoining chapels. The smaller one is dedicated to the Madonna, while the larger chapel has several colourful ancient frescoes: the earliest three are exquisite Byzantine representations. Beyond the crypt, narrow rock-hewn tunnels of tombs wind deep beneath Rabat's streets, including pre-Christian burial chambers complete with intact original skeletons, and later sixth-century Christian additions with frescoes rich in religious symbolism (shells represent heaven; pigeons, the soul; and trees, life). An adjoining and disappointingly outdated museum presents a random assortment of historic artefacts, bones and religious paraphernalia.

Dingli Cliffs

MAP P.66, POCKET MAP D15
Triq Panoramika, Dingli. Bus #56 from Valletta.

This sweep of 250m-high chalky white limestone cliffs plummeting into the cobalt seas is a dizzyingly majestic sight. There are two spots for top views. The humble chapel of St Mary Magdalene, built in 1646, has benches dotted along the clifftop, where you can rest and contemplate Dingli's wild beauty. A pleasant 1.5km walk brings you to Ta Zuta, a headland criss-crossed with well-worn paths, which offers a more expansive view (plus the remains of a Bronze Age wall and silos).

Dingli Cliffs

Cafés

Café Gustav

MAP P.66

3 Triq Il Villagaignon, Mdina
Ⓦ gustavcafe.com.

Boasting terrific views from the highest viewpoint in Mdina, this rooftop café atop the historic Palazzo Falson (see page 68) is a lovely spot to put your feet up and take in views over the Silent City. Enjoy the vistas with a cup of coffee and a traditional Maltese sweet – the *biskuttini tal-lewz* (almond biscuits) are particularly good. €

Fontanella Tea Gardens

MAP P.66

1 Pjazza Tas-Sur, Mdina Ⓣ 2145 0208,
Ⓦ fontanellateagarden.com.mt.

With tables spread out over the parapet of the Mdina fortifications offering dreamy views over Malta, this is a great spot for afternoon tea and cake. It's even better at night, with the fortifications majestically lit and lights twinkling into the distance, when it morphs into a wine bar serving wine, other drinks and platters of finger-food. €

Is-Serkin (Crystal Palace)

MAP P.66

90 Triq San Pawl, Rabat Ⓣ 2145 3323.

An old-style joint, cluttered with Formica tables, offering some of Malta's best *pastizzi* – puff-pastry pockets stuffed with mushy peas or ricotta – as well as hot drinks and alcohol. Cheap and filling, and made with a lard-heavy dough, a couple of *pastizzi* are more than enough. €

Restaurants

De Mondion

MAP P.66

Mistrah il-Kunsill, Mdina
Ⓦ demondion.xaracollection.com.

Cake at the Fontanella Tea Gardens

Part of the five-star *Xara Palace* hotel, *De Mondion* is perhaps Malta's most luxurious dining venue, awarded with a Michelin star and serving lavish dishes such as lobster cannelloni with squid ink or local rabbit pan-seared *en brioche* with pumpkin, king oysters and carob-flavoured rabbit *jus*. The views from its bastion terrace (open summer only) are outstanding. €€€€

Fork and Cork

MAP P.66

21 Telgha tas-Saqqajja, Rabat
Ⓦ forkandwork.com.mt.

Fork and Cork is especially romantic at night, when lights from Malta's southern villages twinkle on the horizon of its small terrace. The food here evokes fine dining but the atmosphere is never fussy. Its seasonal menu rarely disappoints: think rabbit and quail with local figs and radish and Maltese grey meagre fish with bean cassoulet. €€€

Central Malta

Attard, Balzan and Lija – collectively known as the "Three Villages" – are laidback, leafy places, as desirable today as they were when the Knights built country retreats here. Attard's San Anton Gardens – formerly part of a Grand Master's residence – are now Malta's largest and plushest public gardens. Other sites scattered around the villages, which can be seen in a half-day's exploration (there's just a kilometre between each centre), include elegant medieval parish churches, fine old townhouses towering over narrow alleyways and endless delightful Baroque architectural features. Beyond the Three Villages, places of interest include Palazzo Parisio, the swankiest palace open to the public, in the town of Naxxar; and neighbouring Mosta, which boasts one of Europe's largest domes.

Attard

MAP P.76, POCKET MAP E14

The focal point of a visit to **Attard** is **St Mary's Church** (free), set in the compact, quiet and pedestrianized Pjazza Tommaso Dingli. Designed in 1613, the church is regarded as the finest Renaissance church in Malta. Five minutes' walk north, along Triq Il-Kbira and then Triq Sant' Anton, takes you to Attard's other notable sight, **San Anton Gardens**.

San Anton Gardens

MAP P.76, POCKET MAP E14

Triq Birbal, Attard ☎ 2305 3153. Free.

In 1623, the French Grand Master Antoine de Paule built **San Anton Palace** and its **garden** as his private retreat. Today, as the official residence of Malta's President, it is

not open to the public. You can, however, access the large garden, enclosed by high perimeter walls and still retaining the intimate feel of a private estate. The gardens are dotted with oaks, ficus, cypresses, fragrant citrus groves and mature, towering palms. Laid around a grid pattern of cobbled paths, each transverse intersection is decorated with a stone fountain home to turtles, ducks, swans and goldfish. Peacocks and friendly street cats also roam freely.

Ta Qali National Park and Farmers Market

MAP P.76

Ta Qali National Park, Attard. Bus #56 from Valletta, #202 from Sliema or #186 from Buġibba.

For most of the year, Ta Qali National Park (formerly a World

Visiting central Malta

The Three Villages are served by bus #56 from Valletta. From Buġibba, the #186 passes through Mosta en route to the Three Villages, and buses #31 and #41–49 pass through Naxxar to Mosta's town centre.

Mosta Dome

War II RAF station) is not much more than a large dustbowl frequented by joggers or football fans heading for the National Football Stadium within. Its real draw is the chaotic, ramshackle Farmers Market (busiest on Mondays and Thursdays), where you can buy produce directly from more than thirty local farmers alongside Malta's chefs. By law, the produce sold here is the freshest in the country, harvested no more than 24 hours before sale.

Balzan
MAP P.76, POCKET MAP E14

Balzan lays claim to the seventeenth-century **Wignacourt Aqueduct**, built by the Knights to carry water from springs in Dingli and Rabat to Valletta. The aqueduct remained in use until the twentieth century and most of its arches survive today, with the bulk flanking a busy motorway. It's not worth going out of your way for but you're likely to catch a glimpse during a bus ride to Rabat or Mdina.

Lija
MAP P.76, POCKET MAP E14

Lija is an affluent residential neighbourhood that developed from the sixteenth to eighteenth centuries. To see the Three Villages at their most evocative, visit Triq Sant' Anton with its eighteenth-century townhouses (those dating from Malta's British period have rather English front gardens and bay windows) and Triq Sant' Andrija with its seventeenth-century examples. Northwest of Triq Sant' Andrija and west of the main church, a picturesque network of alleyways branches off the winding, bougainvillea-dotted streets. Lija's main square, Misraħ It-Trasfigurazzjoni, is dominated by its 1690s parish church. The square sees one of the best pyrotechnic shows in the world during the town feast each August.

Mosta Dome
MAP P.76, POCKET MAP D14
Triq il-Kbira, Mosta. Free. Buses #31, #41, #42, #44, #45, #47, #48 and #260 from Valletta. Bus #202 from Sliema and #280 from Buġibba.

The nineteenth-century parish church of Santa Marija, better known as the **Mosta Dome**, deserves its place on Malta's tourist trail. Visible from vantage points all around the island, the huge rotunda – claimed to be Europe's third largest – is unlike any other in Malta, designed by architect Georges Grognet de Vasse after the Pantheon. The sacristy is dedicated to recounting the "Miracle of St Mary" when, during World War II, a Luftwaffe bomb pierced the dome during Mass and skittered along the floor without exploding.

Palazzo Parisio

MAP P.76
29 Misraħ ir-Rebħa, Naxxar
ⓦ palazzoparisio.com. Charge. Buses #46, #49, #238 and #260 from Valletta, #203 from Sliema or Buġibba.

This nineteenth-century palace – sole draw of the town of Naxxar – is Malta's most opulent

The greenhouse of Palazzo Parisio, Naxxar

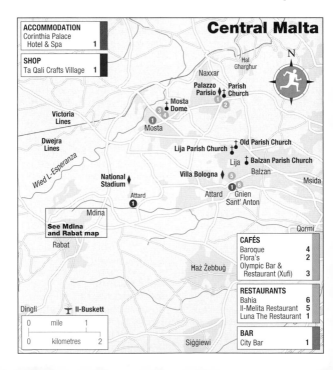

aristocratic home, a fantastic and overwhelming construction of frothy plasterwork reminiscent of a tiny Versailles. Built in the early eighteenth century as a hunting lodge by Portuguese Grand Master Manoel de Vilhena, the palace underwent an extravagant upgrade after Marquis Giuseppe Scicluna acquired it in 1898. Its interior seems plucked out of a fairytale; the Italian artist Filippo Venuti was commissioned to execute the paintings that decorate each room, and gilded Rococo-style stucco carvings blaze across the palace's walls, reaching a garish intensity in the ballroom. After touring the house you can explore the grounds, a green splash of lawns and fountains reminiscent of a British stately home's garden.

Il-Buskett and Verdala Palace

MAP P.76, POCKET MAP D15
Triq Il-Buskett, Il Buskett. Bus #81 from Valletta and Rabat.

Malta's only mature, self-generating woodland, **Il-Buskett** makes a good spot for a stroll or picnic. Created by the Knights in the seventeenth century, Il-Buskett served as the private hunting grounds of Verdala Palace, which was commissioned in 1586 by Grand Master Hugues Loubenx de Verdalle as a country retreat. The palace itself is closed to the public, though you can get a glimpse of its turreted exterior rising above the grove of Aleppo pines that surround it. The woodlands are reached via a snaking road immediately west of the palace, which ends at a car park, from where paths branch in different directions (there are no maps or formal trails). In the peak of summer it's better to give Buskett a miss, as the woodland becomes parched, dusty and punishingly hot. There are no facilities here so bring your own water and snacks.

Dingli Cliffs and Clapham Junction cart ruts

MAP P.76, POCKET MAP D15
Siġġiewi. Bus #62 from Valletta.

Named by British archaeologists after the similarly intricate web of railway lines at Clapham Junction station in London, this jumble of parallel grooves cut into a rocky plateau is the densest network of such ruts in Malta (similar channels are found all over the Mediterranean, but are most numerous here). Archaeologists are unable to date Malta's cart ruts or explain their use. The most accepted – although hazy – hypothesis is that they were made by wheeled carts during the Bronze Age (2000–1400 BCE). However, the ruts have no apparent destination or pattern, disappearing into the sea or halting at cliff-edges. Even the tiny islet of Filfla (see page 101) is webbed with them. The debate on their date and origin continues, with explanations ranging from the simple (they were water channels) to the bizarre (they were made by aliens).

Cart ruts at Misrah Għar il-Kbir

Shop

Ta Qali Crafts Village

MAP P.76

Vjal L-Istadium Nazzjonali, Ta Qali. Hours vary. Bus #80 from Valletta, #65 from Sliema or #66 from Buġibba.

The Maltese traditional crafts sold here are produced in the on-site workshops – many housed in former airplane hangars – and range from ceramics to jewellery. Mdina Glass (ⓦmdinaglass.com.mt) is the highlight of any visit, with free glass-blowing demonstrations. Note, though, that prices overall are lower at the Dbieġi Crafts Village in Gozo (see page 119).

Cafés

Baroque

MAP P.76

13 Church St, Mosta

ⓦfacebook.com/baroquecafemostamalta.

Despite the name, this is a rather modern-looking and pared-down spot (on the inside at least – its surroundings are undeniably Baroque). It's an unpretentious place for a coffee and a light lunch, with a tasty and good-value selection of toasted sandwiches, pizza, waffles, salads and more. €

Flora's

MAP P.76

1 Misraħ ir-Rebħa, Naxxar

ⓦfloras.com.mt.

A positively adorable, sun-drenched tearoom with vintage style, *Flora's* specializes in afternoon tea and cupcakes, and also offers consistently good breakfast and lunch options. €

Olympic Bar & Restaurant (Xufi)

MAP P.76

Triq il-Kostituzzjoni, Mosta

ⓦfacebook.com/xufimosta.

Jam-packed with locals enjoying huge portions of rustic Maltese food plus lots of chatter and banter, the Olympic (more commonly called *Xufi*, the owner's nickname, by locals) is famous for its *ftira* (a roundish ciabatta filled to your liking with tomatoes, cheese, sausage, hard-boiled eggs, onions and olives), acknowledged as some of the best in Malta. €€

Ta Qali Crafts Village

Luna The Restaurant

Restaurants

Bahia

MAP P.76

75 Triq Preziosi, Lija Ⓦ bahia.com.mt.
Bahia won a Michelin star in 2021 for its preservation of local culinary traditions and (too often overlooked) local ingredients with a seasonal menu of flawless old-meets-new dishes. Expect delicacies such as local stone bass *sous vide* in olive oil with heirloom tomatoes, or lamb with *ras el hanout* couscous, homemade falafel and wild-fennel-roasted potatoes. €€€€

Il-Melita Restaurant

MAP P.76

Triq Birbal, Balzan ☏ 2147 0663.
A big family-friendly restaurant offering an array of inexpensive meals such as pies, baguettes, pasta, pizza and even English breakfasts (served until 6pm). It's most pleasant to visit during fine weather, when ample seating is offered in the restaurant's large garden that abuts San Anton Gardens. €€

Luna The Restaurant

MAP P.76

28 Misrah ir-Rebha, Naxxar
Ⓦ palazzoparisio.com.
Located in the extravagant Palazzo Parisio, Malta's very own miniature Versailles, the suitably luxurious *Luna* is best known for its afternoon-tea service. The next best time to visit is for lunch – opt for a table outside to enjoy a classic coronation chicken salad or breaded veal Milanese in view of the palace's fragrant gardens. €€€

Bar

City Bar

MAP P.76

Triq il-Kbira, Mosta ☏ 2143 2080.
A popular, quirky pub located just off Mosta's main square, this fifty-year-old institution offers reliably cheap drinks, always served with free snacks. Owing to its massive popularity with locals of all ages, the pub frequently hosts special events from live music to poetry readings.

The north

The north is the least densely populated area of Malta, characterized by a series of ridges and wide, fertile valleys. Inexpensive accommodation is one draw, particularly in resort town Buġibba; others include the region's multitude of small sandy beaches and family attractions like the Malta Aquarium (see page 82). Development is sparser in Mellieħa, a pleasant, airy town that is the best base in this part of Malta. St Paul's Bay, meanwhile, can refer – confusingly – to both the village of St Paul's Bay and the region that envelops the villages of Buġibba, Qawra and Xemxija. The name is derived from the legend that Saint Paul was shipwrecked on one of the little isles situated nearby. The Knights built a series of watchtowers in the area, including Wignacourt Tower, the oldest surviving watchtower in Malta, but it was not until after World War II that development in this area began in earnest, giving the northern villages their mid-century modern charm.

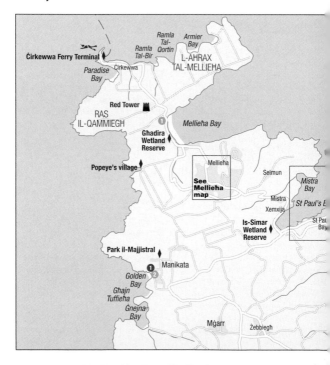

Bugibba

MAP P.84, POCKET MAP F11–G11

Built up in the 1970s as a resort for sun-and-sea package tourism, **Bugibba** is blighted by poor planning and hotchpotch development. The back-to-back apartment blocks and mid-range hotels are dense and dull, but a select few residential streets will transport you back in time with their pretty pastel townhouses and geometric concrete balconies. Cheap rents have resulted in an increasing number of affordable self-catered accommodation and the inexpensive hotels continue to do brisk business, making Bugibba extremely popular amongst retired British expats, young clubbers and tourists visiting for hen and stag dos. Given its good public-transport connections and abundance of restaurants and bars, Bugibba is a viable and convenient base – but you'll want to spend the bulk of your time elsewhere.

National Aquarium

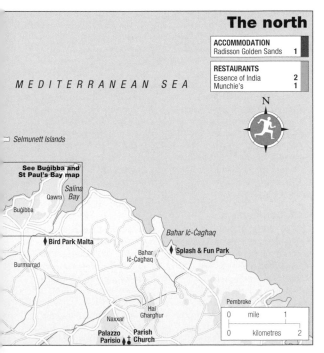

Classic Car Museum

The town's action is mostly concentrated in and around Triq It-Turisti, which is full of tour operators offering excursions round the islands, and the nearby Bay Square (Misrah Il-Bajja), a small, lively pedestrianized plaza fringed by bars, restaurants and cafés.

Qawra

MAP P.84, POCKET MAP G10–H11

Like its bigger sister Buġibba, Qawra is replete with inexpensive, multi-storey three-star hotels, but has fewer bars and restaurants to recommend it. However, the northeastern tip of its shoreline is lined with candy-coloured 1960s villas and boat houses that are worth a quick detour.

National Aquarium

MAP P.84, POCKET MAP H10

Triq it-Trunciera, Qawra Ⓦ aquarium.com. mt. Charge. Bus #45 from Valletta and #212, #222 or #225 from Sliema.
Malta's **National Aquarium**, housed in a beautiful star-fish-shaped building is (like most attractions on the island) compact but compelling. The highlight is the tunnel tank, where horn sharks, dragon eels and cownose rays swim overhead. There are also tanks featuring local fish, with informative displays to help you identify species commonly spotted while snorkelling and swimming off Malta's shores, such as sea bream, sea bass, mullet, grouper, amberjacks and scorpionfish.
A baby station, where different species of fish are bred, is endlessly fascinating – visitors can see eggs and embryos of dogfish, seahorses and sometimes sharks. There are also tropical tanks with puffer fish and clown fish, and a reptiles and amphibians area. The on-site restaurant offers good lunch and dinner options.

Classic Car Museum

MAP P.84, POCKET MAP G11

Tourists Street, Qawra Ⓦ classiccarsmalta. com. Charge. Bus #45 from Valletta and buses #212, #222 and #225 from Sliema.
This 3000-square-metre private museum presents a line-up of pristinely restored T-Birds, Spitfires, Fiats, Alfas, MGs, Jaguars, Fords and other models, alongside antiques and memorabilia from the 1940s to 60s, including

typewriters, gramophones, model toys and period clothes. Restorations are often done live on site in the museum's workshop.

Salina Nature Reserve

MAP P.84

Salina Coast Rd Ⓦ birdlifemalta.org. Charge. Bus #49 from Valletta and #212, #222 or #225 from Sliema.

A former harbour in the Burmarrad valley mouth just east of St Paul's Bay, the Salina Nature Reserve comprises 154,000 square metres of salt pans and marshland, home to a dizzying number of gulls – including black-headed, Mediterranean and Audouin's – terns, sandpipers, herons, and more. The most eye-catching resident is the flamingo. The sight of all these birds wading among flooded salt pans, built by the Knights in the sixteenth century and crowned with towering crosses, is very atmospheric.

St Paul's Bay

MAP P.84, POCKET MAP F11

Follow Buġibba's seaside promenade northwest and you'll encounter **St Paul's Bay village**, with its ribbon of development skirting the coast. Originally a small fishing village, it's tourism that now holds sway here, though the small remaining fleet lends it a picturesque aspect. The seaside promenade is particularly lovely, dotted with towering palm trees.

Wignacourt Tower

MAP P.84, POCKET MAP F11

Tower Road, Buġibba Ⓦ dinlarthelwa.org. Charge. Buses #41, #42 and #49 from Valletta.

Built in 1609 to guard the entrance into St Paul's Bay, **Wignacourt Tower** is one of the largest of the defensive chain built around Malta's coastline by the Knights. A squarish, boxy design, its walls rising solidly to four partly embedded corner turrets, the tower now holds an interesting exhibition that illustrates the Knights' military architecture in Malta with prints of the designs and models of some of the varied defence structures scattered throughout the islands. The first floor recreates the living quarters of the *capomastro* (master

Visiting the north

Transport connections to the north are good but expect at least a 40min ride to Sliema and Valletta. Direct services to Malta's main sights run from Buġibba's tourist-oriented bus station on Triq It-Turisti. From Buġibba, bus routes follow the coast north or south, or venture inland towards Mosta and Malta's fertile valleys. The main routes are #58 to Valletta; #221 to Ċand Mal via St Paul's Bay and Mellieħa; #212 & 225 to Sliema via St Julian's; #223 & 250 to Għajn Tuffieħa and Golden Bay beaches via St Paul's Bay; #186 to Rabat and Mdina; #427 to Marsaxlokk via Tarxien; and #X3 from the airport directly to Buġibba. All buses to Mellieħa pass through St Paul's Bay town centre.

From Valletta, routes #41 and #42 pass through Buġibba and Mellieħa, terminating at Ċirkewwa. #X1 runs from Ċirkewwa through Mellieħa and Buġibba to the airport. All buses bound for Ċirkewwa also pass Għadira Bay beach, Għadira Wetland, the Red Tower and Paradise Bay.

All these services wind down by 11pm, and afterwards a special night service (#N11) operates from Paċeville to Buġibba, Mellieħa and Ċand eħa until 4am.

St Paul's shipwreck

The history of St Paul's Bay is firmly rooted in the story of the saint himself, whom Christians believe was shipwrecked here during his voyage to Rome to stand trial for heresy in 60 CE. To date, no archaeological evidence of the saint's shipwreck has been uncovered. In 2005, a diver discovered a one-tonne lead anchor of the right age and origin in St Paul's Bay, but researchers have been unable to link this anchor to the actual vessel the saint was shipwrecked on, nor have they found any archaeological candidates for the vessel itself. There is also debate over whether, if he did land in Malta, it was in St Paul's Bay or at one of dozens of similar inlets in Malta. Regardless, legend has it that proof of St Paul's miraculous abilities came after he survived a snakebite – Maltese snakes ceased to be venomous thereafter – and he then spent three months converting the Maltese population to Christianity. St Paul's story is now embedded in the national ethos, with the date of the shipwreck, February 10, a national holiday.

A huge statue of St Paul, easily spotted from surrounding villages, dominates the largest of St Paul's Islands, two offshore islets where St Paul's galley supposedly smashed into the rocks. The statue, financed by a local merchant in 1845, depicts St Paul trampling on a snake and brandishing the Bible. Both of the islands are nature reserves dedicated to the protection of a subspecies of the Maltese lizard and Malta's last community of pure wild rabbits.

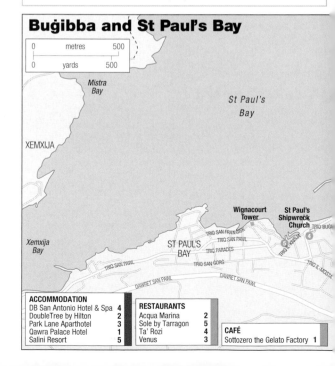

Buġibba and St Paul's Bay

| 0 | metres | 500 |
| 0 | yards | 500 |

Mistra Bay

St Paul's Bay

XEMXIJA

Xemxija Bay

ST PAUL'S BAY

Wignacourt Tower

St Paul's Shipwreck Church

TRIQ SAN FRANĠISK
TRIQ SAN PAWL
TRIQ PARADES
TRIQ IL-KNISJA
TRIQ SAN ĠORĠ
TRIQ SAN PAWL
TRIQ BUĠIBBA
TRIQ IL-MOSTA
DAWRET SAN PAWL

ACCOMMODATION	
DB San Antonio Hotel & Spa	4
DoubleTree by Hilton	2
Park Lane Aparthotel	3
Qawra Palace Hotel	1
Salini Resort	5

RESTAURANTS	
Acqua Marina	2
Sole by Tarragon	5
Ta' Rozi	4
Venus	3

CAFÉ	
Sottozero the Gelato Factory	1

bombardier), who was in charge of the tower with the assistance of two gunners. The soldiers led a plain, rather monastic life here, as evidenced by the undecorated bed, table and benches, and the stone cooking hearth. A staircase leads to the roof, where one of the two original cannons survive, and which affords a lovely view that takes in the entire sweep of St Paul's Bay.

Mistra Bay

MAP P.84, POCKET MAP D10–E11
Buses #41, #42 and #49 from Valletta.
Scenically located at the mouth of a valley that steps up on either side to picturesque terraced fields, horseshoe-shaped **Mistra Bay** is a nice spot for a stroll by the sea. There are no sandy beaches anywhere in the environs of St Paul's Bay and this bay is no different, its shore consisting of a strip of pebbles backed by an access

Mistra Bay

road. The bay is a favourite place for anglers, and on its southern flank a path leads up from the

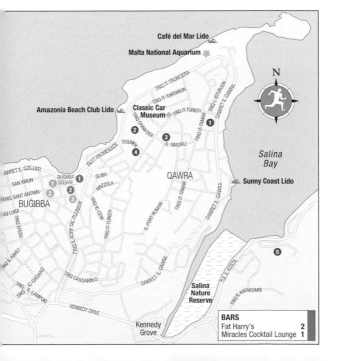

BARS
Fat Harry's 2
Miracles Cocktail Lounge 1

Lidos

The sea around Buġibba and Qawra is clean and clear, but the rocky coast isn't very comfortable for sunbathing. Your best bet is to head to one of the nearby **lidos**, the best of which is **Café del Mar** in Qawra, a splendid modern complex with an infinity pool overlooking the sea, an on-site restaurant offering excellent salads and pizzas, and a fully stocked bar with sunbed service. Entrance here can be pricey, depending on the quality of sunbed you opt for, but drink and food prices are surprisingly affordable. Another option is the leisure club at **Sunny Coast** in the east of St Paul's Bay, which has a pool, café and bar, and the pool at nearby **Qawra Palace**, which offers day passes.

shoreline to a bluff where heaps of boulders tumble down to a clear sea; if you can negotiate getting in and out of the water here you'll be rewarded with good snorkelling among the rocky boulders that string the coast. The impeccably preserved eighteenth-century Mistra Battery sits on the bay's northern flank. Built by the Knights, today it's closed to the public for restoration works, though a short walk around its perimeter walls is worthwhile. The

Mellieħa Church Complex

best time to visit is in the spring; in the height of summer a blight of motorhomes lines the access road, effectively blocking beach access.

Mellieħa

MAP P.89, POCKET MAP C13
Buses #41 and #42 from Valletta, #222 from Sliema and #221 from Buġibba.
Spread over the Mellieħa Ridge, **Mellieħa** has only recently developed any kind of a resort ethic. The fringes of the largely anonymous residential sprawl now bear a peppering of holiday apartments and exclusive villas that cling to its slopes and cliffs, spilling down towards Mellieħa Bay. The narrow, sloping Triq Ġorġ Borg Olivier defines the town centre and holds a smorgasbord of small shops and restaurants. At its northern extremity, Triq Ġorġ Borg Olivier gives way to Triq Il-Marfa, the main artery that snakes down the slope to Mellieħa Bay before cutting across the Marfa Ridge all the way to Ċirkewwa (for the Gozo ferry).

Mellieħa Church Complex

MAP P.89
Parish Square, Mellieħa. Buses #41 and #42 from Valletta, #222 from Sliema and #221 from Buġibba.
Mellieħa's two **churches** sit atop each other at the edge of the Mellieħa Ridge, overlooking Mellieħa Bay. The older of the two

Grotto of Our Lady

is set in the Sanctuary, a lovely courtyard that's accessible from the square (Misrah Iż-Żjara Tal-Papa) via the Monumental Arch, a Baroque stone archway built in 1716. The courtyard is flanked on the right by simple rooms built in the eighteenth century to house pilgrims, and on the left by the **Church of Our Lady of Mellieħa** (free). A squat structure embedded into the rockface, the church began as a crypt and has been expanded twice since the sixteenth century to accommodate the increasing number of pilgrims drawn to the fresco atop the altar, depicting the Madonna cradling Jesus, and said to have been painted by St Luke in 60 CE. The clutter of votive offerings lining the tunnel into the church illustrate the continued belief in the fresco's healing powers, though recent studies have indicated that the saint may not have painted it.

Opposite the Monumental Arch, a second archway and staircase lead up to the bluff that the

larger and newer **Mellieħa Parish Church** (free) stands on. Built in the mid nineteenth century to accommodate the town's growing population, its lean pyramidal dome and bell towers, and its setting at the edge of the ridge, make it a dramatic feature of the skyline. The interior, a bare stone affair with floral carved Baroque motifs, is elegant in its restraint.

Grotto of Our Lady
MAP P.89
94 Ġorġ Borg Olivier St, Mellieħa. Free.
Across the road from the Sanctuary, a small, unmarked doorway from Triq Ġorġ Borg Olivier opens onto a staircase that cuts through an ivy-clogged little valley to the rock-cut chapel known as the **Grotto of Our Lady**, which has existed since medieval times. The only decoration under the softly curved roof is an unremarkable statue of the Madonna enclosed by a metal grille, with a pond fed by an underground spring at its foot; both are said to have miraculous

The Red Tower

healing powers. Many still have faith in the redemptive properties, as evidenced by the candles left by believers, and the votive offerings nailed to the walls.

Air-raid shelter

MAP P.89
Our Lady of the Grotto Street, Mellieħa. Charge. Bus #41 and #42 from Valletta, #222 from Sliema and #221 from Buġibba.
Dug to protect Mellieħa's population during World War II air raids, the town's 500m of underground rooms and tunnels have been opened up as a fascinating, somewhat eerie attraction. Excavated by hand to accommodate upwards of 3000 people, this is one of the largest of such networks in Malta. Some of the rooms are kitted out with mannequins and furniture, giving a tangible impression of the realities of war here.

Ghadira Bay Beach

MAP P.80

Ghadira Bay, a 300m-long stretch of sand lapped by water that is ankle-deep for some 50m out to sea, is Malta's busiest beach. There's parking galore (a main road runs parallel) and good facilities including watersports equipment for rent and a top-notch restaurant. The beach is at its most magical at sunset, when the skyline of Mellieħa is illuminated by twinkling festoons of lights.

The Red Tower

MAP P.80, POCKET MAP C13
Triq tad-Dahar, Mellieħa ☎ 2122 0358. Charge. Bus #41 and #42 from Valletta.
The **Red Tower**, erected in 1649 to supplement the defence afforded by Wignacourt Tower, is colloquially named for the dried-blood colour of its paint job (its formal name is St Agatha's Tower). The tower cuts an imposing, rather fairy-tale figure on the Marfa Ridge, a rugged crest of garigue (a rocky habitat of herbaceous and hardy bushes) interspersed by groves of trees planted during a 1970s reforestation drive. The tower is a boxy construction with outer walls 4m thick, and four mini-towers at each corner. The Knights fitted it with cannons and stationed a brigade of 49 soldiers here, making it the main point of defence in this part of Malta. It was later used by the British as a signalling station during World War II. It's now open to the public, with a short film and somewhat dry informative panels.

Ras Il-Qammiegħ

MAP P.80
Bus #41 and #42 from Valletta.
Beyond the Red Tower, the narrow road that continues west along the crest of the ridge makes for an excellent walk or drive, with wonderful views on either side. Dotted with the stone huts of bird-trappers and hunters, the windswept, scrubby landscape is fragrant with wild thyme, whose

light-purple flowers bloom in late spring (peaking in June). At the head of the ridge, the **Ras Il-Qammiegh** cliffs plummet down dramatically; at the base, boulders as large as churches tumble towards the sea.

Paradise Bay

MAP P.80, POCKET MAP C12
Bus #41 or #42 from Valletta, #222 from Sliema and #221 from Buġibba.

Paradise Bay, a cream-coloured little stretch of sand snuggled into an inlet, is the most attractive of all the Marfa Ridge peninsula's beaches, with clear waters that offer good snorkelling. There are sunbeds, umbrellas and kayaks to rent, a car park and a bar for refreshments.

Popeye's Village

MAP P.80
Triq Tal-Prajjet, Mellieħa
Ⓦ popeyemalta.com. Charge.

The 1980 Hollywood film, *Popeye*, starring Robin Williams, was shot almost entirely in Malta at a purpose-built set – a jumble of colourful buildings overlooking little Anchor Bay – that is now a tourist attraction. Families can make a day of it playing minigolf, visiting the comic-book museum and meeting animators dressed as movie characters. In the summer, free boat trips are offered around the bay, which is lined with sunbeds for parents and floating bouncy castles for tots.

Ġnejna Bay

MAP P.80
Bus #44 from Valletta and #225 from Sliema and Buġibba; transfer to bus #101 at Mellieħa.

Beyond Mġarr (a small, uninteresting town founded in the nineteenth century) the road continues to **Ġnejna Bay**, a large scenic bay nestled in a trough at

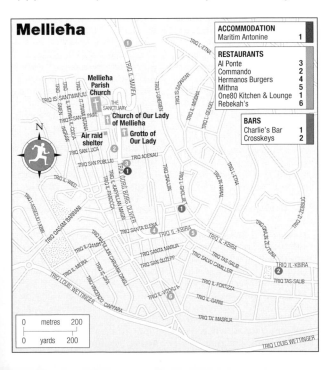

Mellieħa

ACCOMMODATION
Maritim Antonine 1

RESTAURANTS
Al Ponte 3
Commando 2
Hermanos Burgers 4
Mithna 5
One80 Kitchen & Lounge .. 1
Rebekah's 6

BARS
Charlie's Bar 1
Crosskeys 2

the mouth of a valley. The small swath of orange-coloured sand backed by clear, calm water is popular with local families in summer, and mostly undiscovered by tourists. The bay itself is enclosed by dramatic clay slopes crowned by craggy amber cliffs; at the highest vantage point stands one of the Knights' seventeenth-century coastal defence towers.

Għajn Tuffieħa and Golden Bay

MAP P.80, POCKET MAP C13
Bus #44 from Valletta and #225 from Sliema and Buġibba.

North of Gnejna Bay lie Malta's most scenic sandy beaches, divided by a gently rounded peninsula. The southerly of the two, **Għajn Tuffieħa**, is the more dramatic, with the typical clay slopes and cliffs of the coastal landscape hereabouts. A long flight of stairs from the clifftop car park leads to the narrow, crescent-shaped beach, lapped by water that takes on the warm auburn colour of the seabed. During the winter, this is one of the only beaches where surfing is possible; in the summer, the sea is calm and azure. **Golden Bay** is partly spoiled by a multi-storey hotel that dominates the bay from its clifftop perch and, nearer the sand, the road and car park that reach down to the beach. This easier access also means it gets more crowded than Għajn Tuffieħa in summer.

Park il-Majjistral

MAP P.84
Triq Għajn Tuffieħa, Manikata
Ⓦ majjistral.org. Free. Bus #44 from Valletta and #225 from Sliema & Buġibba.

Stretching 6km from the coastal area at Golden Bay beach, **Park il-Majjistral** (Majjistral Nature and History Park) offers excellent gentle hiking, with picturesque views of countryside, cliff and ocean. The park is home to a spectacular diversity of local flora and fauna, including olive and carob trees, myrtle, rockrose and golden samphire. Some 430 different plant species – almost half of the plants known in the whole of Malta – have been recorded to date. Hedgehogs, wild rabbits, Mediterranean chameleons, sparrows and warblers may also be spotted amongst the garigue habitat. On the manmade side of things, you're also likely to encounter remnants of corbelled stone huts (called *giren),* cart ruts, rubble walls, and entrenchments built as part of a coastal defence system by the Knights in the early eighteenth century. Of more recent origin are the World War II pillboxes, a British military barracks and a disused shooting range. The park is most easily accessed through the path that winds behind the *Radisson Blu Golden Sands* resort or by following the signs towards "Haxix Frisk" (fresh vegetables) on Triq in-Nahhalija. After the large dirt car park, turn left onto an unmarked road, where you'll pass a vegetable stand on your way to the park's interpretation centre which offers maps detailing five recommended walks. There are no facilities once you set off, so take your own water.

Splash & Fun Park

MAP P.80
Coast Road, Baħar iċ-Ċagħaq Ⓦ splash.mt. Charge; half-day and multi-day tickets available. Bus #13 from Valletta, #212, #222 and #225 from Sliema, and #222 from Buġibba.

Malta's only **water park** is small and quaint, but offers a pleasant place to spend a day with children. Attractions include a lazy river, a large wave pool and several water slides including the "Sidewinder", "Kamikaze" and the 120m-long "Black Hole". The onsite pizzeria is slightly below average but affordable.

Café

Sottozero the Gelato Factory

MAP P.84

36 Triq Ir-Rebbiegħa, Buġibba

🌐 sottozerofactory.com.

The region's most popular gelato destination, serving traditional Italian flavours. Expect a queue, but it's worth the wait. €

Restaurants

Acqua Marina

MAP P.84

160 St Anthony St, Buġibba

🌐 facebook.com/acquamarinamalta.

Run by a single family, this kitsch, nautical-themed restaurant is arguably the best Sicilian restaurant in all of Malta. If you speak a little Italian, ask your affable host Carlo (the family's elderly patriarch) to fix you a mix of whatever is best that day — expect a multi-course feast of well-priced *antipasti*, pasta, seafood salads, *caponata* and fresh cheeses to miraculously emerge from the restaurant's tiny kitchen. Don't skimp on dessert — the deconstructed *cannoli* are divine. €€

Al Ponte

MAP P.89

94 Triq Ġorġ Borg Olivier St, Mellieħa

🌐 alponterestaurant.com.

A Mediterranean restaurant with classic touches under a rustic vault ceiling with a beautiful terrace, a beautiful wine cellar (housed in a glass-fronted cave) and Italian-inspired fusion dishes. The homemade menu includes pasta, pizza, and mouthwatering deserts. €€

Commando

MAP P.89

1 Misraħ iz-Zjara tal Papa, Mellieħa

🌐 commandorestaurant.com.

A foodie favourite located in front of the picturesque Mellieħa

Mithna

parish church. *Commando* offers seasonal dishes such as local prawn carpaccio with cauliflower and prawn rice croquettes or grilled ribeye with porcini butter and polenta chips. €€€

Essence of India

MAP P.80

1 Misraħ iz-Zjara tal Papa, Mellieħa

☎ 2356 essenceofindia.com.mt.

This high-end restaurant, located at the *Radisson Golden Sands* resort, offers an exquisite gourmet Indian menu served in a beautiful setting atop Golden Bay beach. €€€

Hermanos Burgers

MAP P.89

4 Ġorġ Borg Olivier St, Mellieħa

🌐 hermanosburgers.com.

The best burgers in town are to be found at the ever-popular *Hermanos*, where the food strikes the perfect balance between indulgent and over-the-top — try the Blue Gorgonzola burger, or the New Orleans, stuffed with buttermilk chicken. €

Mithna

MAP P.89

58 Triq Il-Kbira, Mellieħa Ⓦ mithna.com.
A popular Maltese-Italian restaurant offering excellent value for money. The goat's-cheese crêpe with orange-soaked figs and beetroot and traditional slow-cooked pork belly are recommended. €€

Munchie's

MAP P.80

Marfa Road, Mellieħa
Ⓦ munchiesgroupmalta.com.
Malta's best beachside restaurant, *Munchie's* is split over two levels: the lower level offers a casual menu and ambience, and the terrace a larger, slightly more upscale menu. Both offer sweeping views and both menus are delicious, including the picante pizza with spicy chorizo sausage, the home-made pumpkin ravioli, and the generous seafood platter. €€

One80 Kitchen & Lounge

MAP P.89

30 Triq Il-Wied Ta' Ruman, Mellieħa
Ⓦ one80.com.mt.

Located on the beautiful hill below Mellieħa's parish church, *One80* boasts 180-degree views of Mellieħa Bay. Lunch, early and late dinner are served daily with menus that offer a winning blend of comfort food and creativity – think *boullabaisse* arancini and pan-seared tuna salad with lemongrass and coriander salsa. €€€

Rebekah's

MAP P.89

12 Triq it-Tgham, Mellieħa
Ⓦ rebekahsrestaurant.com.
Located on a quiet Mellieħa street in a beautifully restored house of character, *Rebekah's* offers a perfect taste of contemporary local cuisine and old-world charm. The pork cheeks, risottos, *tortellaci* and fresh fish are all top notch. The restaurant also graciously caters to vegetarian and gluten-free requests with food that is no less superb than the rest. €€

Sole by Tarragon

MAP P.84

St Julian's, St George's Bay
Ⓦ tarragonmalta.com.

Fat Harry's pub

By one of Malta's most renowned chefs, *Sole by Tarragon* offers Mediterranean fare with a firmly modern twist at surprisingly good prices. Indulge with cold foie gras pate bonbons dipped in chocolate and hazelnuts or venison and pistachio ravioli tossed in honey and coffee crème fraiche. €€€€

Ta' Rozi
MAP P.84
96 Church street, Buġibba ☎ 2157 1411, Ⓦ tarozirestaurant.com.
A fantastic Mediterranean seafood restaurant off the beaten path. You can enjoy excellent dishes, like pan-seared quail with honey and *baccheri* with Maltese sausage, from the beautiful terrace. €€

Venus
MAP P.84
Triq Il Gandoffli, Buġibba
Ⓦ venusrestaurantmalta.com.
Run by a local family, this charming restaurant harnesses the rich bounty of the Maltese coast and countryside to whip up tempting dishes like veal ribeye on the bone with chimichurri, seafood risotto, and rabbit ravioli. The catch of the day is always a good bet, and don't forget to leave room for the daily-changing dessert menu, which showcases traditional Maltese sweets. €€

Bars

Charlie's Bar
MAP P.89
Triq il-Hasira, Mellieħa ☎ 2152 2010.
A quirky British-run hole in the wall where the drinks are cheap and the crowd is cheerful. Cards and board games are made available, and there's even a small swimming pool. Bingo nights are hosted on Tuesdays (book ahead). €

Crosskeys
MAP P.89
5 Cross Square, Mellieħa ☎ 2152 3744.

One80 Kitchen & Lounge

Despite its rather dated decoration, *Crosskeys* is very popular with locals, British expats and tourists. British-style roasts are available on Sundays. €

Fat Harry's
MAP P.84
Pjazza Walkway, Buġibba
Ⓦ fatharryspub.com.
Located just off Buġibba's main square, *Fat Harry's* makes a decent stab at authentic pub decor and offers a fantastic atmosphere, plus a varied menu of pub grub and drinks. €€

Miracles Cocktail Lounge
MAP P.84
Bay Square, Buġibba
Ⓦ facebook.com/miraclesloungemalta.
A very popular lounge bar on Buġibba's lively main square serving cocktails by the glass or pitcher alongside sharing platters and burgers. Miracles shows major sports matches and has extensive outdoor seating. €€

The south

Malta's least-touristy region consists of a clutch of old towns and seaside villages that have retained a measure of traditional Maltese life now absent from the more commercial north. Most distinctive are Żejtun and Marsascala. The former is a self-possessed old-style town whose charm comes mostly from its atmosphere, although it does also have an exceptional church. The latter is a sleepy seaside village that has largely escaped the development of resorts and high rises, and has a lovely seaside promenade and rocky beach to recommend it. Undoubtedly the most famous village in the south is Marsaxlokk, where a daily open-air market draws crowds to purchase fish fresh from the traditional, brightly painted *luzzu* boats moored nearby.

The south is also home to a few small beaches and Malta's finest four **Neolithic temples**, all World Heritage sites, ranging from the underground Hypogeum to the enormous temples set atop tumbling coastal cliffs near Wied Iż-Żurrieq. **Accommodation** options in the south are limited to self-serviced apartments, so most

Tarxien Neolithic temples

visitors chose to stay in Valletta, Sliema/St Julian's or Buġibba and venture south for day-trips.

Tarxien Neolithic temples

MAP P.96, POCKET MAP E15–G15
Triq it-Templi Neolitici, Tarxien
ⓦ heritagemalta.mt. Charge. Buses #82, #84, #85 and #88 from Valletta.

The largest and most architecturally advanced temple complex in Malta, the **Tarxien Neolithic temples** are among the last built on the island, sometime between 3000 and 2500 BCE. Evidence of fires here suggests that Bronze Age people used the buildings as a crematorium. For millennia the complex lay buried under an accumulation of rubble until it was discovered by a farmer in 1914. What survives now is the bottom third of the temples; the building, when intact, stood some 23m high. The Tarxien complex comprises three interlinked temples. Entry is through the South Temple, where the first chamber holds a grand altar with spiral reliefs and a replica of the bottom half of Malta's iconic "Fat Lady" sculpture (the original is in the National Museum of Archaeology; see page

3). When whole, it would have measured 2.5m high, making this the largest of these figures found anywhere in the world. The Central Temple's symmetrical chambers contain evidence of arched roofing, and if you look closely at a chamber to the right you can see faded but breathtaking motifs of marching bulls and goats carved on the megaliths. Only a bottom foundation stone survives of the East Temple, but a number of altars found here (now at the National Museum of Archaeology) contained flint knife and animal bones, meaning animal sacrifices probably took place here.

Hal Saflieni Hypogeum

MAP P.96, POCKET MAP E15
Triq iċ-Ċimiterju, Paola
ⓦ heritagemalta.mt. Charge. Buses #82, #84, #85 and #88 from Valletta.

The **Hal Saflieni Hypogeum** is one of the oldest and most impressive monuments of the ancient world. This extensive underground shrine was cut into soft globigerina limestone over three levels between 3600 and 2500 BCE, and was still a work in progress when Malta's Neolithic settlers disappeared without trace. It was only rediscovered in 1899, and today the full purpose of the Hypogeum remains a matter of conjecture and debate. It was certainly connected to funerary ritual, but the fact that only seven thousand bodies were recovered here – which means just seven burials per year over the thousand years the Hypogeum was in use – suggests that only priests or priestesses were laid to rest here. Whatever the Hypogeum's exact

Addolorata Cemetery, Paola

function, it's a unique structure with a tangible air of mystery, and you really do have to see it to appreciate its profoundly stirring atmosphere.

Tours (45min) of the complex start with an audiovisual presentation, and proceed with an audio-guide tour supervised by watchful tour guides. You begin on the first (and oldest) level, where an intact entrance trilithon (two upright megaliths with another laid on top) creates a gateway into the underground realm. Archaeologists believe the second and most ornate level is where funerary processions began. It is daubed with spiral representations in evocative red ochre, perhaps representing the Neolithic people's worldview of cyclical continuity. An incomplete

Visiting the south

The attractions in the south are fairly scattered but can be reached by bus. Routes #80–94 (most depart from Valletta) service the south via Marsaxlokk, Tarxien and Żejtun. After 11pm, the #N10 night bus runs from Paċeville to Marsascala and Żejtun until 4am.

Visiting the Hypogeum

Only eighty people are allowed in each day, so visits need to be planned well ahead – bookings (through 🌐 heritagemalta.mt) are often full months in advance. If all else fails, you might still get a place on one of eight special daily tours – these are available only as last-minute tickets and can be purchased the day before from the National Museum of War (Fort St Elmo, Valletta) and the Gozo Museum of Archaeology (Victoria).

section here illustrates how the complex was dug out, first by boring holes using deer antlers, then knocking off chunks of rock between the cavities with stone mallets, and finally polishing and painting the walls. It was in the main chamber of the second level that the iconic "Sleeping Lady" figurine was recovered (see page 33). Further on, the **Oracle Room** is decorated by a painted tree thought to symbolize the tree of life; the room itself takes

its name from the Oracle Hole, a niche which, when spoken into, amplifies voices into echoes that boom through the underground space (similar to the Oracle of Delphi). The purpose of the room known as the Holy of Holies remains a mystery, as no bones were recovered during excavations. In front of its entrance, two linked holes in the ground may have been used to collect libations or solid offerings. The third and youngest level is a complex of smaller spaces

RESTAURANTS

Diar il-Bniet	2
Tal Familija	3
Tiny Mint Bistro	1

reaching 10m underground, which served as mass graves.

Addolorata Cemetery

MAP P.96, POCKET MAP E15

Vjal Santa Lucija, Paola. Free. Buses #1–4, #80, #82 and #88 from Valletta.

Consecrated in 1869, Malta's largest burial ground, **Addolorata Cemetery**, is worth exploring for its Neogothic architecture and collection of bombastic Baroque-styled tombs. From the entrance, a path meanders uphill past elaborate marble-cased tombstones (their hotchpotch of designs is bewildering and beautiful) overhung by cypress, olives, carobs and Aleppo pines. At the highest reaches of the cemetery, the well-to-do are laid to rest inside sumptuous mausoleums. The Gothic Revival chapel at the top of the hill is closed to the public, but the ornate exterior is noted for its (rare in Malta) stained-glass windows.

Church of St Catherine, Żejtun

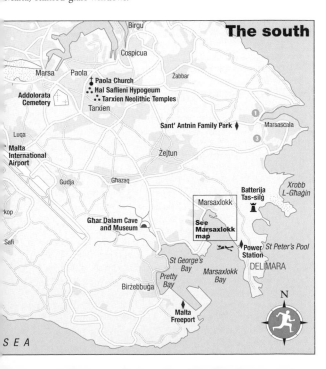

Addolorata Cemetery also contains 250 Commonwealth burials from World War I and eighteen from World War II.

Żejtun

MAP P.96, POCKET MAP F15

Bus #80, #82, #85 and #88 from Valletta.

One of the great pleasures of visiting Żejtun is strolling about its quiet sun-dappled streets, soaking up the atmosphere. The town has prospered since Phoenician times, and its name – which means "olive" in Arabic – is evoked today in the annual olive festival, the best time to visit. The village's highlight is St Catherine's Church, designed by Lorenzo Gafa in 1692, which dominates the skyline for miles around. The surrounding streets are littered with medieval architectural features, and the most distinctive building, situated near the bus station on Misraħ Carlo Diacono, is Aedes Daniels Palace with its imposing facade bedecked with large statues. Adjacent are two medieval chapels, and along their southern flank runs Triq Luqa Briffa, which leads east to the town's old quarter, where you'll find a maze of twisting alleyways and delightful architectural details.

Marsascala and St Thomas Bay

MAP P.96, POCKET MAP F15

The seaside village of Marsascala, well off the tourist track, offers a pleasant taste of everyday life in Malta. Situated on a peninsula that divides two bays, it has evaded the over-development of the central

Neolithic Malta

Malta's **Neolithic community**, which blossomed from 5000–2500 BCE, was the most advanced civilization of its time. Its temples (almost 25 major sites have been discovered so far) are the oldest freestanding man-made structures in the world and the relics within are more artistically sophisticated than anything found elsewhere of the same period. Yet Neolithic Malta remains shrouded in mystery.

Malta is thought to have supported between 5000 and 10,000 Neolithic inhabitants, and most of that number must have been working on the megalithic temples given the mobilization required to build them – yet the people also had to produce food and build domestic homes. Generations of archaeologists have pored over this contradiction, which is complicated by the fact that in around 2500 BCE the Neolithic community came to an inexplicable and sudden end. The most mainstream explanation is that the inhabitants over-exploited the environment and, with their natural resources dwindling, became obsessed with religious salvation from their predicament. Critics argue that there is no supporting evidence of environmental distress and the erection of the temples is in itself a sign that the people had abundant resources. Another theory holds that Malta was much larger at the time, and what survives is the tip of its mountain, on which most of the temples are concentrated. There is geological plausibility in this: the Pantelleria Rift, southwest of Malta, constantly produces upwarping of the land, and this could have led to a massive earthquake that destroyed the larger part of Malta and its inhabitants. However, there is no hard proof for this or any other theory. The mystery continues.

Mnajdra Neolithic temple complex

and northern regions. No surprise, then, that the village has attracted Malta's bohemians and artists, who have opened alternative bars and restaurants along Marsascala Bay. A palm-lined promenade snakes from here along the peninsula's perimeter, from which you can see saltpans cut into the shoreline. At the tip of the peninsula stands **St Thomas Tower**, built by Grand Master Alof de Wignacourt in 1614 to protect the southern coast from corsairs. The promenade continues to **St Thomas Bay**, a popular summer swimming spot with good facilities, where chalky white cliffs slope into shallow water.

Sant' Antnin Family Park

MAP P.96, POCKET MAP D15
Triq Sant Antnin, Marsascala. Free.
Malta's largest **leisure park**, built to rehabilitate a closed landfill, offers a pleasant (and free) diversion for families. The park is home to a picnic area, playgrounds, outdoor gym, rock climbing, dog park, olive grove, football pitch and equestrian area, as well as a petting zoo with goats, llamas, ponies and chickens.

Parking is free; bring your own snacks and water.

Ħaġar Qim and Mnajdra Neolithic temples

MAP P.96, POCKET MAP D15
Triq Ħaġar Qim, Qrendi
ⓦ heritagemalta.org. Charge. Bus #74 from Valletta.
Situated on a rugged and scenic rocky plateau that reaches down to the area's dramatic cliffs, the **Ħaġar Qim** and **Mnajdra Neolithic temple complexes** – constructed between 3600 and 2500 BCE – are Malta's most atmospheric outdoor temples. Sitting less than a kilometre apart, they are a deeply stirring sight – despite the transparent protective shields that were put up in 2008 to protect them from weather erosion.

Visits begin at the excellent visitor centre, which shows a 4D film experience that documents the site's history, from Neolithic construction to discovery in the nineteenth century. Several interactive exhibitions provide a good overview of the possible construction techniques and uses of the temple complexes, with fun interpretation material provided for children.

Ħaġar Qim, a circular complex of four temples, where spaces and chambers open into each other in an intricate jumble of rooms, is the least understood of all Maltese temple sites. The understanding of these spaces, and their ceremonial significance, is close to nil. No burial remains have been discovered, although animal sacrifices may have taken place, but most theories do point to a religious purpose: in the rear of one apse, a curious series of low stone slabs form an inner enclosure. On the summer solstice, the sun's rays pass through a small elliptical hole to dramatically illuminate one of the slabs.

A 500m walk along a gently inclining path brings you to the Mnajdra complex, three temples that form a continuous concave facade. At the Central Temple look for the architectural plan carved into one of its megaliths at the time of construction; this is claimed to be the first ever architectural design. The elegant South Temple is the best preserved of any on the Maltese islands. Its main entrance is decorated with small drilled holes to mark the position of the rising sun on the equinoxes and solstices. In its first chamber you'll find the so-called Oracle Hole, a small aperture that opens into a hidden cubicle that's thought to have been the seat of a hidden oracle, who may have passed on messages or interpreted epiphanies during ceremonies. Only the foundations survive of the East Temple.

Wied Iż-Żurrieq and the Blue Grotto

MAP P.96, POCKET MAP E15
Bus #38 or #138 from Valletta. Charge for boats to Blue Grotto.

Enclosed by a deep gorge and lying at the mouth of a creek, most

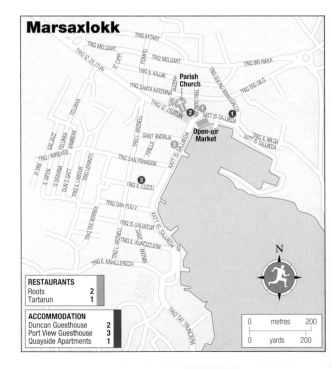

Marsaxlokk

RESTAURANTS
Roots · 2
Tartarun · 1

ACCOMMODATION
Duncan Guesthouse · 2
Port View Guesthouse · 3
Quayside Apartments · 1

people come to the former fishing outpost of **Wied Iż-Żurrieq** to board one of the boats that ferry visitors to the **Blue Grotto** and other smaller caves. The Blue Grotto is a dramatically domed cave opening at sea level, fronted by a buttress eroded into the rocks. The sea within has a deep-blue luminosity, especially in early morning. That said, the wait to get a boat can be hours' long, their drivers aren't particularly affable and the constant boat-traffic ruins the atmosphere.

Filfla

POCKET MAP D16

Filfla is a tiny uninhabited islet located 5km offshore. Its name is believed to come from *felfel,* Arabic for peppercorn. Sadly, until 1971, the British Royal Navy and Air Force used the island for target practice (spent cartridges are still being found today) reducing the island's size and turning its cliffs into mounds of rubble. Since 1980 it has been designated a nature reserve (off limits to the public) in an effort to protect its large colony of storm petrels and its endemic species of wall lizards and door snails.

Marsaxlokk

MAP P.100, POCKET MAP F15
Bus #81 and #75 from Valletta or #TD11 from Sliema and Buġibba.

Marsaxlokk is a must-see on any southern itinerary. Set around the

Marsaxlokk

deep scoop of Marsaxlokk Bay, it is home port for Malta's largest fishing fleet, and the spectacle of the town's fishermen and their colourfully painted *luzzu* (wooden boats) remains its principal allure. Marsaxlokk's seafront promenade serves as its town centre, with its church and pedestrianized square set by the shore. At its daily open-air market here hawkers (literally) sell everything under the sun, including some excellent Maltese lace, local olives, honey and fresh seafood (look for octopus, squid,

Traditional Maltese fishing boats

Demanding great skill to build, traditional *luzzu* are more expensive now than modern fibreglass boats, but most fishermen prefer them for their stability and durability. Fishing here reaches its zenith during the late summer and autumn: the fishing season for lampuki (dolphin fish). Lampuki are uniquely fished using the *kannizzati* method, which has not changed significantly since Roman times. Fishermen cut and gather the large palm fronds and weave them into flat rafts, which are pulled out to sea by *luzzu*. At midday, lampuki schooling under the rafts seeking shade are netted. The eyes painted on the prows of *luzzu* are supposed to lead fishermen to their catch.

St Peter's Pool

swordfish, tuna, and sometimes even shark). The most popular day to visit is on Sunday morning when the market is at its biggest and busiest. Most restaurants here cook delectable, fresh fish (see page 103). Booking ahead is a must, especially on Sundays in the winter when locals descend for long, leisurely seafood lunches.

St Peter's Pool

MAP P.96, POCKET MAP F16
A 30min walk from Marsaxlokk (not advised in the hot summer months).

At scenic **St Peter's Pool** the shore is sculpted by winter storms into a combination of dramatic cliff faces and – the major draw – a crescent-shaped swimming hole cut into the golden limestone. The clear water is an ideal spot for a dip, and some sections of the smooth limestone shores are comfortable for sunbathing. Depending on wind conditions, there can be an issue with unsightly flotsam: it's advisable to visit when the wind is blowing from northern or westerly directions, or when it's dead calm. There are no facilities at St Peter's Pool; bring your own water and snacks.

Għar Dalam Cave and Museum

MAP P.96, POCKET MAP F15
Għar Dalam Road, Birżebbuġa
Ⓦ heritagemalta.mt. Charge. Bus #80 and #82 from Valletta.

Although billed as a major sight, **Għar Dalam Cave and Museum** is of minor appeal. The cave is considered the place where Malta's human story began, so the site should be fascinating, but the dusty Victorian-style exhibits here are mostly limited to bones. Excavations of the 145m-deep cave (only 50m of which are accessible to visitors), mostly carried out following its discovery in 1892, yielded human teeth and a skull that were dated to 7000 years ago, making them Malta's earliest human remains. Other finds include the remains of prehistoric animals, such as hippopotamus and dwarf elephants, flushed into the cave at the end of the last Ice Age, back when the level of the Mediterranean was considerably lower than it is today and Malta was connected to Europe via land bridges.

Pretty Bay

MAP P.96
Bus #X4 from Valletta.

As its name suggests, **Pretty Bay** is very easy on the eye, boasting Malta's most tropical-looking beach, with soft white sand and glistening turquoise waters. The only catch is that it overlooks Malta's massive Freeport – the twelfth busiest in Europe. To put a positive spin on things, it can be fascinating to lie back on the beach and watch the massive tankers unload – the contrast is memorable.

Restaurants

Diar il-Bniet

MAP P.96

Triq il-Kbira, Dingli W diarilbniet.com.
Alongside *Tal-Petut* in Birgu (see
page 53), *Diar il-Bniet* offers
the best taste of Maltese rural food
on the island. Everything here,
down to the cheese and olive oil, is
handmade with ingredients grown
on the restaurant's 600-acre farm.
The menu changes seasonally, and
typically includes rustic farmhouse
pies, gourds stuffed with spiced
minced beef, and deliciously sweet-
and-sour aubergine *kapunata*. €€

Roots

MAP P.100

67 Xatt is-Sajjieda, Marsaxlokk
☏ 2165 3205.
Located on Marsaxlokk's seafront
promenade, *Roots* is a lovely spot
to watch the colourful fishing
boats bobbing in the harbour as
you feast on juicy steaks, pasta
dishes, or seafood – the squid
tempura, mussel soup with rice,
and octopus carpaccio are highly
recommended. €€

Tal Familija

MAP P.96

Triq il-Gardiel, Marsascala

Seafood in Marsaxlokk

W talfamiljarestaurant.com.
An airy restaurant spread across
three intimate dining areas,
specializing in homely Maltese
cooking with an emphasis on fresh
fish and shellfish and typical Italian
pastas. €€

Tartarun

MAP P.100

29 Xatt is-Sajjieda, Marsaxlokk
W tartarun.com.
Fresh line-caught fish are the
star of the show at *Tartarun*,
where chefs put creative twists on
traditional recipes using seasonal
ingredients. Think black tortellini
with local prawns and crabs in
a fermented honey veloute or
langoustine served with preserved-
citrus couscous. €€€

Tiny Mint Bistro

MAP P.96

3 Triq ix-Watt, Marsascala
W facebook.com/tinymintbistro.
A small, no-frills restaurant
popular with locals, with an
emphasis on fresh fish and other
seafood – the mussels are justly
acclaimed, while the prawn pasta
and seared tuna steaks have much
to recommend them, too. Best
enjoyed with a crisp glass of
white wine, on an outdoor table
overlooking the water. €€

THE SOUTH

Gozo

Gozo offers a delightful mix of historic attractions and rural tranquility, with a dramatic coastline dominated by headlands and large bays in the north, and a girdle of cliffs interspersed with gorges in the south. The slow and easy pace of life here is irresistible, while the island is increasingly on the radar of outdoor-sports enthusiasts, offering superb scuba diving, rock climbing, canoeing and hiking. Gozo may not seem all that different from its sister island but spend a little time here and the contrasts become apparent: sleepier villages clustered around deep, verdant valleys of handsome terraced hills; and low-slung townscapes that blessedly lack Malta's high-rises.

Entertainment mostly revolves around cafés by day and restaurants in the evening, the latter serving hearty Gozitan dishes alongside Italian classics.

There are only a dozen or so hotels in Gozo, concentrated in the seaside towns of Marsalforn and Xlendi. Most people stay in luxuriously converted farmhouses

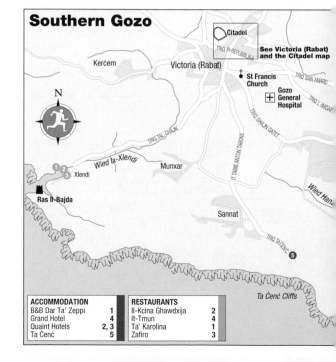

ACCOMMODATION	
B&B Dar Ta' Zeppi	1
Grand Hotel	4
Quaint Hotels	2, 3
Ta Ċenċ	5

RESTAURANTS	
Il-Kċina Ghawdxija	2
It-Tmun	4
Ta' Karolina	1
Zafiro	3

GOZO

for B&Bs in smaller villages across the island. The Gozitans themselves are affable, close-knit, deeply religious and justifiably proud of their little island. Although locals are outnumbered year-round by tourists, they are renowned for their warm hospitality.

Victoria

MAP P.106, POCKET MAP B11

Gozo's pleasant capital, **Victoria** (in Maltese, Rabat, though easily confused with Malta's own village of the same name), is dominated by the Ċittadella and defined by its main thoroughfare, Triq ir-Repubblika (Republic Street), which cuts across the town. Here you'll find the island's largest concentration of shops, Gozo's main theatres (the Astra and Aurora) and the Villa Rundle Gardens, a little haven of shade in the summer heat and the stage

for outdoor concerts during summer months. However, it's the old part of town that holds the most charm, its maze of alleys lined with pretty townhouses, elaborately carved stone balconies and niches containing Catholic icons. The area is quiet and pedestrianized, bounded at the north by Pjazza l-Indipendenza, a tree lined square laid out in front of the Banca Giuratale, an unusual circular Baroque building from 1733 that is now the town hall. The morning tourist market in this square offers kitsch souvenirs, but the cafés (see page 120) surrounding it have outdoor tables that are great for soaking up the scene and the sunshine. The square adjoins Pjazza San Ġorġ to the south, dominated by the ornate **St George's Basilica** (free), the most sumptuously Baroque of Gozo's churches.

SHOP	
Vini e Capricci	1

BAR	
Gleneagles	1

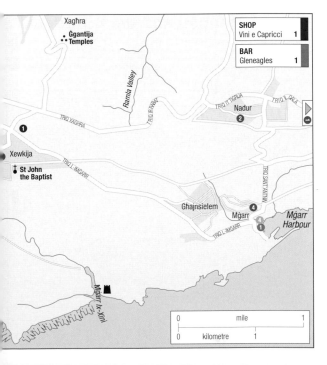

GOZO

The Ċittadella

MAP P.106, POCKET MAP B11
Free.

Gozo's bulwark **castle**, commanding a ridge overlooking Victoria, is the island's oldest settlement and on the list to become a UNESCO World Heritage Site. The visitor centre, housed in a nineteenth-century water cistern at the base of the citadel, is unmissable, offering an excellent 360-degree documentary film experience.

The Ċittadella, which traces its beginnings to 2500 BCE, was under the control of various occupying forces until a City Council was established in the fourteenth century. By the time the Knights arrived in 1530, over five thousand people were living in the Ċittadella. In 1551 nearly all of them were dragged into slavery when Ottoman corsair Dragut Rias laid siege. After this disaster, the City Council put forth a contentious regulation requiring all remaining Gozitans on the island to sleep in the Ċittadella between May and October, when the calm seas were rife with corsairs. The regulation was not repealed until 1637.

The main attraction of the Ċittadella is **Gozo Cathedral**, which was designed by the celebrated Maltese architect Lorenzo Gafa and built between 1697 and 1711. Funds ran out before the cathedral's dome was built, so the interior of the "flat dome" now features a spectacular *trompe l'oeil* painting of a false dome. The **Cathedral Museum** at the back of the church (separate entrance on Triq Fosos) holds a disorienting jumble of the church's historic artefacts; if you're pressed for time, it's easily skipped.

The other focus points of a visit to the Ċittadella are its four **museums**, only two of

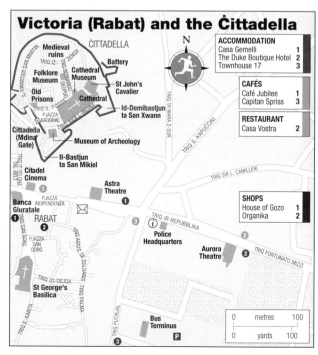

which are worth checking out (ⓦheritagemalta.mt; charge; combined tickets available, including those for all Heritage Malta Gozo sites/museums).

The first of these is the **Archaeology Museum**, a small repository of relics discovered in Gozo, spanning all periods from the Neolithic to the Arabic era and detailing the discovery of the Ġgantija temples and the priceless ancient artefacts found within. Top exhibits include the fascinating and voluptuous Neolithic stone figurines that would be at home in any contemporary art museum, amulets representing Egyptian deities found in the limits of Xewkija and, from the Arabic epoch, a marvelous marble tombstone with a long and poetic dedication.

Gozo was used as a place of exile since antiquity, when Byzantine emperor Heraclius (610–641 BCE) sent his conspiring son Theodorus to die here. The sixteenth-century **Old Prison** is Gozo's last site of exile and the Ċittadella's other notable museum. The most famous inmate here was Jean de la Valette (the Grand Master at the time of the

Cathedral of the Assumption

Great Siege, for whom Valletta was named), who was imprisoned for four months for attacking a layman. Today, the prison cell walls bear the graffiti left by former inmates, which was discovered when a layer of lime whitewash was removed during rehabilitation works. Frequent motifs include the outline of a palm (akin to a signature), galleys, calendars and even games.

Visiting Gozo

The main link between the islands is provided by 24hr **ferries** (ⓦgozochannel.com; every 45min in daytime, every hour at night; 25min) between Ċirkewwa in Malta and Mġarr Harbour in Gozo. Foot-passenger tickets and car/driver tickets are both available. Gozo's main **bus** station is on Triq Putirjal in Rabat, with buses calling at most of Gozo's towns from 5.30am to 11pm. You can get a bus schedule from the tourist office on Triq Ir-Repubblika in Victoria, or at ⓦpublictransport.com.mt. You can pick up **taxis** at the Mġarr ferry terminal or at Victoria's bus terminal and Independence Square. White taxis (equipped with meters) can be hailed. For private cars and airport transfers try Mayjo Car Rentals (ⓦmayjocarhire.com). Double-decker hop-on hop-off **tour buses** cover all major tourist sites. Street **parking** around Gozo is free and ample (look for spaces marked in white). Rabat also has two large free car parks located several blocks apart on Triq Giorgio Borg Oliver. Next to the main entrance of the Citadel there is also a small private paid car park.

Victoria, the capital city of Gozo

The **Folklore Museum** holds mildly diverting implements of traditional trades, the largest of which is a mule-driven wheat mill. The building itself, a medieval Siculo-Norman house that's full of nooks and crannies, is more interesting than its contents. The fourth and final museum, the **Natural History Museum**, is of marginal interest, with panels illustrating Gozo's geology, as well as some ad-hoc displays dedicated to flora and fauna, including a depressed flock of dusty, stuffed birds.

Visiting the Citadel's museums is not essential to appreciating this ancient site but wandering the length of its **ramparts** absolutely is. A stroll is enriched by the free Ċittadella app (Ⓦ visitgozo.com), which provides a custom audio tour based on your location within the fortress.

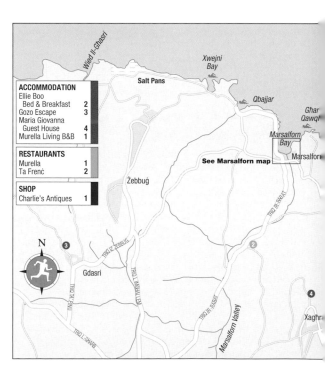

ACCOMMODATION
Ellie Boo
  Bed & Breakfast   **2**
Gozo Escape   **3**
Maria Giovanna
  Guest House   **4**
Murella Living B&B   **1**

RESTAURANTS
Murella   **1**
Ta Frenċ   **2**

SHOP
Charlie's Antiques   **1**

Wied Il-Għasri
Xwejni Bay
Salt Pans
Qbajjar
Għar
Qawql
Marsalforn
Bay
Marsalfor
See Marsalforn map
Żebbuġ
N
Gdasri
Xagħr

TRIQ TA' ĊAWL
TRIQ IZ-ŻEBBUĠ
TRIQ IL-GĦARB
TRIQ L-IMĠARR IX-XINI
TRIQ IL-BARAT
TRIQ JR-BARAT
Marsalforn Valley

Xewkija

MAP P.104, POCKET MAP B11–12

Bus #323 and #301 from Victoria.

The main reason to visit **Xewkija** – one of the oldest villages in Gozo – is to see the massive **St John the Baptist Church** on Pjazza San Ġwann Battista (free), whose dome is visible from all over Gozo. The Baroque design is by the Italian Giuseppe Damato, inspired by the Basilica of Santa Maria Della Salute in Venice. Its dimensions are impressive: supported by eight internal pillars, the honey-coloured 75m-high dome is the tallest in Gozo, while the building's internal volume is only slightly smaller than St Peter's Cathedral in Rome. It's an awe-inspiring structure, built over a forty-year period with the donated funds of the faithful and the donated time of local skilled craftsmen.

Mġarr Ix-Xini

MAP P.104

Bus #301 from Victoria.

The signposted road from Xewkija to **Mġarr Ix-Xini** (which is rough but safely passable) meanders past cattle farms along the south flank of the dramatic **Ħanżira Valley**, a gorge cut into the bedrock by an ancient river – now a popular spot for rock-climbing. The valley meets the sea at Mġarr Ix-Xini, a tranquil fjord fronted by a small patch of pebbly shore, where the transparent water beckons you for a dip. Mġarr Ix-Xini translates as "the harbour of the galleys", referring to the time when it provided a hidden anchorage for corsairs' frequent raids on Gozo. Nowadays, its beauty attracts yachts to drop anchor but, absent from the usual boat tour circuit, the bay is a relatively hidden gem (for now, at least). At the mouth

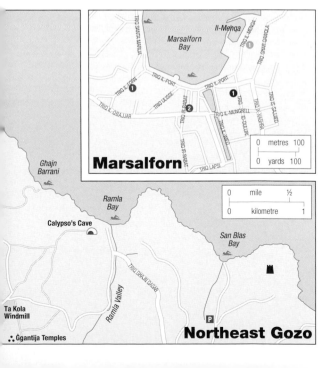

of Mġarr Ix-Xini lies the largest **coastal watchtower** erected in Gozo, whose construction by the Knights in 1658 effectively deterred the activities of marauders. An old cobbled path leads from the bay to the tower, which is operated by heritage NGO Wirt Ghawdex and is open to the public on Saturdays (open whenever the flag is flying; free).

Ta Ċenċ Cliffs

MAP P.104, POCKET MAP B12
Bus #305 from Victoria.

Just outside the nondescript town of Sannat, the land falls sharply into the sea at **Ta Ċenċ**. With sweeping views of the sea stretching towards the horizon, it's a very scenic spot for a walk (there are no picnic facilities or bathrooms, so take your own water); the rocky *garigue* (a rugged habitat of hardy bushes) supports some interesting local fauna and flora. Clumps of rock centaury – Malta's national plant, with small, succulent leaves and fluffy mauve flowers in summer – cling to the cliff edge, and the area is a favoured haunt of the blue rock thrush, the national

bird, easily identifiable by its dark brown or blue plumage and habit of flicking its tail feathers up and down. Ta Ċenċ is best known, however, for its one thousand or so pairs of Cory's shearwaters that nest in crags on the cliff face when they're not spending the day at sea. As one of the largest colonies in the Mediterranean, they make this an Important Bird Area (IBA) according to BirdLife International.

Xlendi

MAP P.104, POCKET MAP A11–12
Bus #306 from Victoria.

Xlendi, a picturesque seaside village, is an essential stop on any Gozo itinerary. Top billing goes to the compact waterfront, which fronts a pebbly beach lined with cafés and restaurants, and is popular for long, leisurely lunches – especially on Sundays when extended Maltese families catch up over heaving plates of food – although it is under threat from controversial planned tower-block developments. Xlendi is a designated swimming zone during the summer, and also offers excellent snorkelling and diving.

Xlendi at night

Canoes and paddleboats, a great way to explore the bay's many caves, are available to rent at the small wharf. From the wharf, a white staircase ascends the great limestone hill that long made Xlendi bay a favourite refuge for ships since Roman times (a large number of amphora have been found on the seabed in the mouth of the bay). Head up and over the hill to reach Caroline's Cave, formerly the property of a wealthy woman from Victoria who donated it to the local Augustinian nuns so they could enjoy their very own secluded swimming hole. Continue west along Xlendi's promenade for delightful views of the sheer cliffs on Gozo's southern coast, which until a few generations ago were favoured by the area's so-called "climbing fishermen", who inched down to ledges near the bottom to fish in the deep waters. This path, built by the Knights, leads to the coastal Xlendi Tower at the mouth of the bay, built by Grand Master Juan de Lascaris-Castellar in 1650 as a defence against corsairs.

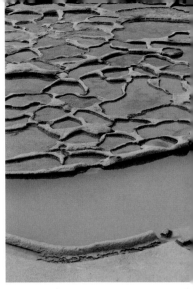

Xwejni saltpans

Marsalforn

MAP P.108, POCKET MAP B11
Bus #310 from Victoria.

On the opposite northern coast from Xlendi, **Marsalforn** is Gozo's largest seaside resort, consisting of a ribbon of inexpensive apartment blocks and small hotels spread across a large bay, particularly popular with British tourists and retirees. Despite its mass of buildings, the bay has an open feel and for much of the year it feels like a resort in low season – only on summer evenings does a bustle of strollers build and the seafront restaurants fill up. There's some traditional colour at Il-Menqa, a small breakwater-enclosed harbour on the east flank of the bay that's the docking station for a dwindling number of brightly painted *luzzi* fishing boats; otherwise, there isn't much else to distract you from lounging by the sea. During the summer, you can swim at a small sandy beach at the inner mouth of the bay; most locals prefer to swim off the rocks that trace the waterline along the west side of the bay, where the promenade gives way to the rocky shoreline (there are ladders for getting in and out).

Xwejni saltpans

MAP P.108
Bus #310 from Victoria.

Gozo's **saltpans** – a web of geometric depressions gouged into the soft yellow globigerina limestone – take up a 2km by 50m strip of the island's coastline. During winter, heavy waves splatter seawater over the rocks to fill the pans; this evaporates during the summer, leaving thick crusts of crystal salt. If you visit in August, you'll see gangs of workers shovelling the salt into bags; the uncrushed crystals are sold in most local supermarkets. The pans are beautiful, particularly during winter, when the reflection of the sky in the water-filled pans makes it look like a field of mirrors.

Wied Il-Għasri

MAP P.108, POCKET MAP A11
Bus #309 from Victoria.

A deep, snaking gorge some 300m long with a creek at the bottom, **Wied Il-Għasri** (Għasri Valley) is reached via the right fork of the road beyond the last saltpans, or from the village of Żabbar via a short hike down Triq is-Saghtrija. A flight of stairs pickaxed into the side of the cliff leads to the inner mouth of the creek and a tiny pebbly shore. This is an excellent spot for diving and snorkelling in the summer; look out for rays, deep-water fish and some curious underwater topography towards the outer reaches of the creek.

Xagħra

MAP P.108, POCKET MAP B11
Bus #307 from Victoria.

One of Gozo's largest towns, **Xagħra** sprawls over a series of ridges and bluffs. It's a comparatively busy place, with an attractive and lively town square, Pjazza Vittorja (Victory Square), fringed by oleander trees and handsome Baroque townhouses abutted by old colonial-era bars.

At the head of the square stands the Church of the Nativity of Our Lady, a fine example of an eighteenth-century village church, with its ornate bell towers, dome, and an overwhelmingly gold-and-crimson interior.

Ġgantija temples

MAP P.108, POCKET MAP B11
Triq John Otto Bayer, Xagħra
Ⓦ heritagemalta.mt. Charge. Bus #307 from Victoria.

Of all the Neolithic temples in the Maltese islands, the two at **Ġgantija** are perhaps the most evocative and impressive; they're also the oldest freestanding man-made structures in the world, erected around 3600 BCE and predating Stonehenge and the Egyptian pyramids. The word Ġgantija derives from the word Ġgant (giant), since the Gozitans used to believe the temples were built by a race of giants – when you see the size of the limestone blocks here, you might well agree. This complex of temples laid under an accumulation of rubble for thousands of years before being discovered and excavated in 1827.

Xagħra

Since then, erosion has taken a heavy toll, but the half-ruined edifice remains an imposing sight with its megalithic walls projecting over the bluff it's situated on – the largest megalith, weighing 55 tons, is as big as a lorry. The circular complex comprises two temples, and their form and layout, as well as the artefacts found within them, suggest they were an important ritual focus of a highly organized society. Remains of animal bone and stone hearths point to rituals involving animal sacrifices. A number of libation holes in the floor may have been used for the pouring of liquid offerings, and decorated features found inside the temples include patterns of drilled holes and bas-relief panels depicting spiral motifs, trees, plants and various animals. The complex is accessed through an Interpretation Centre, built to accommodate the 200,000 tourists who visit the site every year. It's worth lingering here to learn more about daily life in the Neolithic period and the theories on how the temples were constructed and used, besides viewing a fascinating selection of prehistoric artefacts found on Gozo.

Ta Kola Windmill

MAP P.108

Triq Il-Mithna, Xagħra ⓦ heritagemalta.org. Charge. Buses #64 and #65 from Victoria. The oldest surviving **windmill** built by the Knights is now open as a tourist attraction, having ceased commercial wheat-grinding at the beginning of the twentieth century. When the wind was right for the mill to operate, the miller would blow through a triton-shell (in Maltese, *bronja*) to let villagers know to bring their grain to be ground into flour. The original, intact apparatus that turned the grinding stones is still in situ: a complex series of huge cogwheels fashioned entirely out of timber. On the upper floor, the millers'

Calypso's Cave

recreated living quarters offer a view on daily rural life in Gozo, including a kitchen decked out with a traditional *kenur*, a stone hearth used for stewing.

Calypso's Cave

MAP P.108, POCKET MAP B11
Bus #302 from Victoria. On foot, take the path from Ramla Bay beach. By car, go via the village of Xagħra; you've arrived when you reach a small car park and gift shop.
Perched on a bluff above the sea, **Calypso's Cave** is (misleadingly) touted as the legendary grotto inhabited by the nymph Calypso in Homer's *Odyssey*, where she kept Odysseus captive through love for seven years. In Homer's work, that grotto was on an island called Ogygia and, although evidence exists that Gozo was once called Ogygia, the proof that this is the true Calypso's Cave is circumstantial (muddling things further, some researchers also claim that the real cave is situated in a valley in Mellieħa). The unimpressive cave itself, formed

GOZO

by fissures in the rock surface, is closed to the public due to unstable geological movement. However, a viewing platform offers a gorgeous scene of clay slopes tumbling down to the orange sand of Ramla Bay and rolling inland into Ramla Valley – you can pick out the town of Nadur on a ledge at the valley's far side.

Ramla Bay

MAP P.108, POCKET MAP B11
Bus #302 from Victoria.

Enclosed by twin headlands, little **Ramla Bay** is among the most stunning beaches in the Mediterranean. Set at the mouth of a large valley and flanked by high ridges, the beach is a strip of soft, bright orange-coloured sand that gives way to a sweep of clear shallow sea. At the back of the beach, the sand rises into dunes that are bound by tamarisk trees – the only sand-dune habitat

in the Maltese islands, and home to rare plants and insects (avoid lying or walking here). The bay also holds two historical attractions: an underground wall built by the Knights to hinder enemy boats from landing and, on the eastern flank of the bay, a *fougasse* – a rock-cut mortar that was designed to be filled with rocks and gunpowder and fired on enemy vessels attempting to break through the underwater wall. Ramla is attractive at any time of the year – it's a great spot for a stroll in winter, and the best beach in Gozo for swimming in the summer – but it gets understandably crowded in July and August, especially on Sundays. For a quieter spot, there's a small sandy creek on the western flank of the bay, reached via a ten-minute walk from the beach proper along a path that skirts the shoreline. Parking is on the wide access road and private fields that are turned

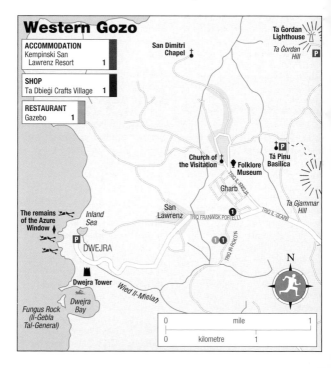

Western Gozo

ACCOMMODATION
Kempinski San Lawrenz Resort — 1

SHOP
Ta Dbieġi Crafts Village — 1

RESTAURANT
Gazebo — 1

Ta Ġordan Lighthouse
Ta Ġordan Hill
San Dimitri Chapel
Church of the Visitation
Folklore Museum
Ta' Pinu Basilica
Gharb
Ta Ġjammar Hill
The remains of the Azure Window
Inland Sea
San Lawrenz
TRIQ FRANWISK PORTELLI
TRIQ IL-KNISJA
TRIQ IL-GEBEL
TRIQ IR-ROKON
DWEJRA
Dwejra Tower
Wied Il-Mielaħ
Fungus Rock (Il-Ġebla Tal-Ġeneral)
Dwejra Bay

N

0 — mile — 1
0 — kilometre — 1

Ramla Bay

into a temporary car park in the summer; just before the beach, a couple of operators rent umbrellas and sun loungers. Kiosks serve drinks and snacks, and old-school ice-cream trucks occasionally drop by. There are also public toilet and shower facilities available.

San Blas Bay

MAP P.108, POCKET MAP C11
Bus #303 from Victoria.

San Blas, a small, sandy beach with red-orange sand, is like a miniature version of Ramla. It has been left in its pristine natural state, and the only commercial activity is a portable kiosk where you can rent umbrellas and sun loungers, or have a drink and snack (mostly chips and burgers, but sometimes fresh prawn and calamari if you're lucky). It's a scenic spot for a day by the sea, snorkelling in its shallow water or sunbathing. The downside of San Blas's natural glory is limited access: unless you're driving, you have to walk for half an hour from Nadur's town centre. Even if you're driving, the farmers' access road is a narrow concrete strip that is closed to traffic from halfway down

because it is exceptionally steep. During high season, privately owned Jeeps offer rides up and down the hill (you can negotiate better rates for a group). Portable toilets are offered during the summer months but expect fewer facilities in the winter.

Ta' Pinu Basilica

MAP P.114, POCKET MAP A11
ⓘ 2155 6187. Free. Bus #308 from Victoria.

A couple of kilometres west of Rabat lies the imposing **Ta' Pinu Basilica**, Gozo's primary pilgrimage site. The church had its beginnings as a medieval chapel, but by 1575 had fallen into disrepair and was marked for demolition. However, the worker who struck the first sledgehammer blow apparently broke his arm – an incident interpreted as a divine sign, which led to the chapel being spared. In 1883, legend has it that Ta' Pinu gained more notoriety when a local fieldworker, Karmela Grima, heard a disembodied voice summoning her to the chapel to "recite three Hail Marys in honour of the three days my body was confined to the tomb". Grima's story spread

Ta' Pinu Basilica

like wildfire, and islanders began following the voice's call. The present church was built between 1920 and 1932 to accommodate the ever-increasing number of pilgrims who still visit today. The handsome church itself is set in the midst of open countryside overlooking a terraced green valley. Its limestone interior is packed with ornate stone sculptures, but most interesting is the original medieval chapel itself at the back of the present church. The corridors on either side of the altar that lead to the chapel are cluttered floor to ceiling with votive offerings (crutches, braces, shoes, framed photographs, and letters of devotion from around the world) left by those allegedly healed by the church's miracles. Opposite the church, the Stations of the Cross have been reproduced with life-size marble statues lining a route up the Ta Ghammar hill – a popular pilgrimage route, especially during Easter. The view from the top of the hill, which takes in northwest

Gozo's motley sweep of fields and compact towns, is worth the walk.

Għarb

MAP P.114, POCKET MAP A11
Bus #312 from Victoria.

Għarb is the most traditional village in Gozo. It's also the sleepiest. Until recently, it was populated almost exclusively by people who worked the surrounding fields and retained an old Maltese dialect, with a vocabulary of words and pronunciations long since discarded by the rest of the population. Lately, it has attracted second-home buyers and many of its buildings are now converted into luxuriously rustic villas. The swimming pools and landscaped gardens haven't detracted from Għarb's appeal, though, with its pretty streets and expansive vistas. The village's **Church of the Visitation**, located in Pjazza taż-Żjara, was completed in 1732 and boasts an unusual and striking concave facade. Take a short walk outside of the village

Fungus Rock

Fungus Rock became renowned in the eighteenth century following the discovery of a parasitic plant that was thought to have medicinal and mythological powers. By 1746, the Knights had put the rock under 24-hour guard to preserve the plant for the privileged use of European rulers. Science eventually discounted the alleged medicinal properties, but the rock remains out of bounds to protect the tuber's only habitat in Malta. Phallus-shaped and covered in tiny, velvety brownish-red flowers, the plant's resemblance to a mushroom earned it the (incorrect) common name of "Malta Fungus". It grows abundantly here but is relatively rare elsewhere in the world.

towards the coastal cliffs to visit the tiny, charming chapel of St Demetrius. A longer hike on the road along Wied il-Mielah brings you through the fertile Gozitan countryside (a sea of yellow Cape Sorrel flowers in the spring) to the sea, where you can find **il-Mielah Window**, Gozo's "other Azure window" – all the more appealing since its big sister disappeared during a storm in 2017. The sea below, only accessible by boat, is an outstanding dive site. With Gharb village known for its skilled craftsmen and lace makers, it's

worth checking out the nearby Ta' Dbieġi Crafts Village (see page 119).

Dwejra

MAP P.114
Bus #311 from Victoria.

Dwejra is most famous for what is no longer there. The iconic **Azure Window**, a picturesque natural opening in the cliffs some 100m in height and width, was lost to rough seas during an intense winter storm in 2017. The window was created by wave erosion over the centuries – a process that had significantly

Inland Sea, Dwejra Bay

Fungus Rock (also known as General's Rock)

accelerated in recent years – and ultimately destroyed by the same forces. The loss of the Azure Window was deeply mourned by Gozitans and anyone who was lucky enough to see it in person. However, Dwejra still has plenty to recommend it, with distorted, crater-like topography that makes for some very scenic walking. Offshore, the underwater cliffs, valleys, massive plateaux, coral-supporting caves and – nowadays – the remains of the Azure Window offer excellent scuba diving (see page 144).

The bus from Victoria drops you at a car park near the **Inland Sea**, a landlocked body of seawater connected to the Mediterranean via a tunnel in the towering cliff face. In the opposite direction, southeast of the car park, another path takes you to **Dwejra Tower**, part of the coastal defence chain built by the Knights. Beyond the tower is the horseshoe-shaped **Dwejra Bay**, at whose mouth **Fungus Rock** (*Il-Ġebla Tal-Ġeneral*) – the result of a partial seabed collapse over 23 million years ago – soars 70m out of the sea into a stout pinnacle.

Gozitan *ftiras*

Traditional Gozitan pizzas (called *ftiras*, but not to be confused with the Maltese bread of the same name) are still made by two bakeries in Nadur town. Traditionally, *ftiras* came in two forms – either topped with anchovies, tomatoes, onions and potatoes or as closed pizzas stuffed with sheep's cheese beaten into eggs – but now most bakeries have introduced other varieties. Best of Nadur's two bakeries is *Maxokk Bakery* (21 Triq San Gakbu, ⓦ maxokkbakery.com), where the bready *ftiras* are cooked in a wood-fired oven. If you prefer a dough that's easier on your teeth, go to *Mekren's Bakery* (Triq Ħanaq, ⓦ facebook.com/mekrensbakery), which does larger *ftiras* with a crumblier dough. If you're not able to get to Nadur, try the less authentic but passable *ftira* at Kcina Ghawdxija in Xlendi, with its pie-like crust.

Shops

Charlie's Antiques

MAP P.108

Triq id-Duluri, Marsalforn
🌐 facebook.com/Charliesantiques.

Offers a delightfully odd
assortment of vintage bric-a-brac
and World War II paraphernalia,
including shell casings, Victorian
prams, traditional wooden
Gozitan lace bobbins and heaps
of funky film cameras. Unlike
most thrift shops, *Charlie's* is
meticulously organized, making
it easy to find one-of-a-kind
souvenirs.

House of Gozo

MAP P.106

28 Triq Sir, Victoria
🌐 facebook.com/houseofgozo.

A modern souvenir shop selling
beautiful souvenir art prints,
handmade greeting cards and
postcards of Gozitan landmarks.

Ta Dbieġi Crafts Village

Organika

MAP P.106

13 Pjazza San Ġorġ, Victoria
🌐 organika.com.mt.

An eclectic shop where the focus is
on fairtrade and organic products
(primarily jewellery, clothing,
art pieces, chocolates and teas)
ethically sourced from around
the world, as well as affordable
souvenirs such as local sea salt.

Ta Dbieġi Crafts Village

MAP P.114

Triq Franġisk Portelli, San Lawrenz
🌐 gozoartisans.com.

A cluster of artisan workshops
producing and selling good-quality
and relatively inexpensive local
crafts such as ceramics, leather
goods, Maltese lace, wool sweaters
and filigree jewellery.

Vini e Capricci

MAP P.104

Gozitano Agricultural Village, Triq l-Imġarr,
Xewkija 🌐 viniecapricci.com.

Café Jubilee

A superb selection of fine Italian charcuterie, a large wine cellar, and several Gozitan artisan food brands make this an ideal place to load up on delicious souvenirs.

Cafés

Café Jubilee

MAP P.106
Pjazza l-Indipendenza, Victoria
Ⓦ cafejubilee.com.

This café-bar attracts regulars for its coffee and daytime snacks, becoming more of a quiet bar with good music in the evenings. You can't go wrong with a local lager and *pastizzi* – theirs are the best on the island – or the superb rustic ravioli for lunch. €

Capitan Spriss

MAP P.106
66 Main Gate St, Victoria Ⓣ 2156 9112.

A charming Italian café on Victoria's busiest street that is excellent for breakfast, with fresh croissants and proper Italian coffee. €

Restaurants

Casa Vostra

MAP P.106
62 Republic St, Victoria
Ⓦ facebook.com/CasaVostraGozo.

With a trendy interior and a superb menu of traditional Italian food, *Casa Vostra* gets rave reviews from locals and visitors alike. The pizzas are superb – try the one topped with nduja, aubergines, and yellow tomatoes – and rich pasta dishes, burgers and salads round out the offerings. There's a good selection of Gozo-brewed craft beer, and the homemade *limonata* is also not to be missed. €€

Gazebo

MAP P.114
Triq ir-Rokon, Kempinski Hotel
Ⓦ kempinski.com.

Located in the lush gardens of the *Kempinski Hotel*, the romantic *Gazebo* restaurant is only open during the summer and serves a superb selection of local seafood enhanced with locally foraged herbs such as sea asparagus from Dwejra. For turf rather than surf, try the homemade violet potato gnocchi with asparagus, pine nuts and pecorino. The minted melon with orange blossom ice cream and lime fizz dessert is as delicious as it is fun. €€€

Il-Kcina Ghawdxija

MAP P.104
Xatt ix-Xlendi, Xlendi Ⓣ 2156 9118.

You'll pay more to experience traditional Gozitan fare here than in a typical village restaurant, but the view of Xlendi Bay is worth it. Try the Gozitan rabbit stew, grilled pork chops served with eggs, or a *ftira*, akin to a pizza, filled with beaten eggs, fresh local cheese and potatoes. €€€

t-Tmun

MAP P.104

Triq Martino Garces, Mġarr
tmunrestaurant.com.

In operation for over 25 years,
Tmun has established an excellent
reputation with locals for its
upscale but hearty cuisine served
in an elegant, nautically themed
atmosphere. The *bouillabaisse* with
calamari, prawns and shellfish,
and whole fresh fish *al sale* (baked
in salt), are house specialities.
€€€

Murella

MAP P.108

Triq il-Menqa, Marsalforn
facebook.com/murellagozo.

A relaxed family restaurant set on
the seafront in Marsalforn serving
pasta, wood-fired pizza, grills and
salads. For a taste of local flavours,
try the Gozitan *ftira* (see page
118). €€

Ta Frenċ

MAP P.108

Triq Għajn Damma, Victoria tafrenc.mt.

The excellent *Ta Frenċ* serves rich
French cuisine in a converted
Gozitan farmhouse. Expect the
likes of foie gras with *creme brulée*
glaze, veal gel, grilled quail breast
and toasted sourdough or (at the
upper end of the scale) the house
omelette with lobster, mushroom,
leeks and a lobster bisque sauce.
€€€€

Ta' Karolina

MAP P.104

Triq l-Għar ta Karolian, Xlendi
karolinarestaurant.com.

Perfectly sited restaurant on the
waterfront in Xlendi, overlooking
the harbour. *Ta' Karolina's* menu
leans towards seafood, as you
might expect given its setting –
the mussels in white wine and
garlic sauce are superb, as is the
marinated octopus – but there is
also a good selection of land-based
offerings, including braised rabbit,
and great pizzas. €€€

Zafiro

MAP P.104

Xatt ix-Xlendi, Xlendi zafiro.mt.

A fairly upmarket (but very
affordable) restaurant on Xlendi's
promenade where homemade pasta
and fresh seafood are the stars of
the show. The mussels, *fritto misto*
and *garganelli* pasta are particularly
hearty and delicious. The best
seats are outside overlooking the
turquoise sea. €€

Bar

Gleneagles

MAP P.104

10 Victory St, Mġarr Harbour 2155 6543.

Opened in 1885, this former
fishermen's watering hole is
decorated with nautical curios
and has a friendly, small-town
feel. The tables set on the balcony
afford good views of the colourful
harbour.

Ta Frenċ

Comino

Though it looks like little more than a barren, sun-baked rock from the sea, tiny Comino (just 2km long by 1.7km wide) offers breathtaking clifftop scenery, two of the Maltese islands' most scenic swimming spots, and great snorkelling and diving. The island is a car-free nature reserve and virtually unpopulated, with only two permanent inhabitants and nowhere to stay – although controversial plans are underway for two new hotel developments including an ultra-luxe *Six Senses* resort slated for 2027. More plentiful than human residents are feathered ones; the island is a haven for migratory birds and birdwatchers, since hunting and trapping are forbidden year-round.

From June to September, Comino sees its fair share of visitors and the area around the Blue Lagoon becomes very congested, since a dip in its crystal-clear waters is not to be missed. Shoulder season (October to May) is an ideal time to explore the island by foot, when the rocky habitat blooms into a mosaic of flowers and milder temperatures make hiking comfortable (avoid venturing out in the extreme heat of summer as Comino is nearly treeless and devoid of shade).

Blue Lagoon

Visiting Comino

The **Comino Ferries Co-Op** (Ⓦcominoferries.com) operates year-round shuttles between Malta's Ċirkewwa ferry terminal or Marfa Resort and Comino's Blue Lagoon or Santa Marija Bay. The shuttles run every 30min in the summer and hourly in the winter. Check the website for up to date ferry times.

Ebsons (Ⓦcominoferryservice.com) also operates a ferry service between Mġarr (Gozo; see page 104), the Blue Lagoon (Comino) and Ċirkewwa (Malta).

The **standard fare** for trips with all companies is €15 return (discounts are usually offered for larger groups). From November to February boats operate sporadically due to low demand, so it's best to call ahead.

Several **tour companies** operate regular trips to Comino from April to October, most stopping in Comino for five hours, which is plenty of time to swim and explore. Captain Morgan is the most popular choice among backpackers, with rock bottom prices (Ⓦcaptainmorgan.com.mt; ticket includes lunch and free bar). Hornblower Cruises are a more comfortable option, with an a/c lounge, basic café facilities and a rooftop lounge area with waterslide (Ⓦhornblowerboat.com).

The island has been populated at least since Roman times (a full archaeological survey of the island has yet to be undertaken) and was a popular hideaway for corsairs during the time of the Knights, but it was likely most highly populated during Malta's brief French occupation (1798–1800) when the island served as a place of exile and imprisonment for at least 150 criminals and opponents of the regime.

The Blue Lagoon
MAP P.124, POCKET MAP C12

A sweep of bright turquoise water sandwiched between Comino and its sister islet of Cominotto, the **Blue Lagoon** is aptly named. The water is crystal clear, and you can enjoy the dramatic vista of the cliffs and Comino's tower as you swim between the islands, but be advised of strong rip currents here yearlong, and lifeguards are only on duty between June and October. The downside is that the Blue Lagoon gets hideously overcrowded in summer, when boats packed with

day-tripping tourists anchor in the bay from mid-morning until late afternoon. The small patch of sand fronting the lagoon at both ends is riny and fills up quickly, and even on sunny winter afternoons some touring boats call at the lagoon. If you're looking for quiet, it's best to visit in the morning on one of the first tour boats of the day. Public toilet facilities are available, and in the summer a number of food trucks offer snacks and ice creams.

St Mary's Tower
MAP P.124, POCKET MAP C12
Free.

The sheer cliffs and variegated colours of the deep waters beyond the Blue Lagoon serve as a beautiful backdrop to **St Mary's Tower**. The largest of the Knights' coastal towers, with walls over 5m thick, the tower was built in 1618 by Grand Master Alof de Wignacourt as a base for the garrison of troops stationed on Comino to protect the island from invasion and to guard the Malta–Gozo channel. From its roof you can see almost the entire

Santa Marija Beach

Santa Marija Bay

MAP P.124

With inviting turquoise water and a small strip of sand, **Santa Marija Bay** is an ideal alternative to the Blue Lagoon and locals' preferred option for a beach day in Comino. There's good snorkelling among the rocks towards the outer reaches of the bay, and sunbeds and umbrellas can be rented from the kiosk on the beach, which also offers refreshments and shower facilities. There's also a free public campsite between the beach and nearby chapel (follow the signs posted). On the other side of the headland that encloses the bay (and not accessible from land) is a popular **dive site** known as Santa Marija Cave, renowned for its silvery shoals of docile bream, which are happy to eat stale bread from your hands like pets. All Gozo-based dive centres (see page 144) organize trips to the site.

island. Film buffs may recognize St Mary's Tower as Château d'If from the 2002 Hollywood film, *The Count of Monte Cristo*.

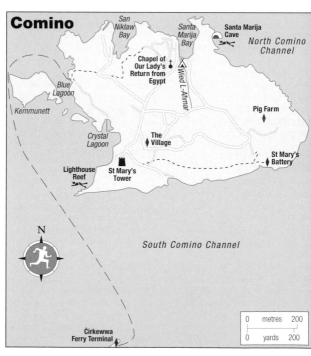

A Comino walking tour

This circular route around Comino, departing from Blue Lagoon in an anti-clockwise direction, takes about two hours. Keep your eyes peeled for wildlife including Maltese wall lizards, wild rabbits and Mediterranean chameleons (not found on Gozo and Malta). You might also come across chunks of rusting iron – reminders that the British used the island for target practice in the early twentieth century.

To begin, head off in the direction of **St Mary's Tower** (see page 123). The path on this part of Comino passes by a string of attractive islets, the **Crystal Lagoon** and Comino's only valley – il-Wied ta' Skalanova. Venture off route into the valley and you'll find a 20m-wide hole in the rocky ground. This is a collapsed limestone cave, called the **Roofless Cave**, the entrance to which can only be seen from the sea. Passing St Mary's Tower you will see **il-Palazz** (the Palace), formerly a colonial-era isolation hospital for plague and cholera victims. By 1948 it housed a community of 65 people who grew export crops on Comino until the early 1960s (you can still see the rubble walls dividing disused farming fields across the island)

Turning right, follow the road constructed by the Knights to connect St Mary's Tower and St Mary's Battery. Erected in 1714, the latter is the best-preserved of the dozens of batteries erected by the Knights in their drive to reinforce Malta's coastal defences. The garigue habitat here supports a hugely diverse array of plants, including musty scented wild thyme and capers, which sport beautiful white-and-purple blooms in spring. Continue straight along Comino's southern coast to arrive at the defensive battery, where the path turns north and leads to **Wied l-Aħmar (The Red Valley)**, fringed by native carobs, olives, almonds and Aleppo pines; in the spring, the uncultivated portions of the valley are covered with a carpet of bright yellow Cape Sorrel flowers.

As the valley widens, a pink-coloured outpost built by the Knights in 1743 (now housing Comino's police station) and a diminutive thirteenth-century **chapel** (Our Lady's Return from Egypt) come into view. Shaded by cypresses and a palm tree, and with timber doors and three bells dangling inside stone hoops, the simplicity of its design – typical of medieval Malta's vernacular architecture – gives the building a striking, evocative appearance. The chapel overlooks **Santa Marija Bay** (see page 124) – continuing along the road beyond the chapel you can turn right at the first crossroads to go to San Niklaw Bay, or press on and return to the Blue Lagoon.

St Marijo Tower

ACCOMMODATION

InterContinental Malta

Accommodation

Hotels and guesthouses book up several months in advance, especially in high season. The average rate for a good four-star hotel in Malta begins at around €100, and more luxurious options start at €200. The cheapest hotels are in the north, and the most expensive around Sliema, St Julian's and Valletta, which also offer the best transport links. Except in Valletta, most hotels (and some self-catered options) have parking. Unless stated otherwise, all places listed are for the cheapest online double room rate in high season, including breakfast and en-suite facilities; low season rates would be less than half this. Malta's hostels are quickly catching up to (and often exceeding) its hotels in modern amenities and chic style. The majority are located in Sliema and St Julian's, and are typically a third of the price of even the most affordable hotels (dorms from €20 and double rooms from €50). Most organize group activities and excursions, and many have outdoor pools (where barbecues are hosted during summer nights). Unless stated, prices include breakfast. Self-catering accommodation is a good-value option for groups and families. You'll find budget options in the south and north, and (comparatively) more expensive options in Valletta, Sliema, St Julian's and Gozo. Particularly in Gozo, minimum stay lengths (2–5 days) usually apply. Along with the places listed below, try Airbnb or, for Gozo (where farmhouses are the most popular self-catered option), try ⓦ gozoholidayhomes.com or ⓦ gozovillas.com.

Valletta

CASA ELLUL MAP P.28, POCKET MAP E6. 81 Old Theatre St, Valletta ⓦ casaellul. com. Malta's most exclusive boutique hotel, discreetly located in a Victorian palazzo opposite the Carmelite Church (see page 37), with eight personalized suites designed by young Maltese architect Chris Briffa. Rooms have luxurious touches throughout; expect two-storey ceilings, walk-in showers, espresso machines, Maltese balconies, breathtaking bathtubs and one-of-a-kind antiques. Two suites facing the church's impressive dome boast private terraces with jacuzzis. €€€€

HOTEL CASTILLE MAP P.28, POCKET MAP E7. St Paul St, Valletta ⓦ hotelcastillemalta.com. The 38-room *Castille* is conveniently located between Auberge de Castille and Upper Barrakka Gardens. Rooms are charming, with exposed limestone walls, and most offer lovely piazza views. Facilities include lounges, a restaurant and a beer cave. €€

LA FALCONERIA MAP P.28, POCKET MAP E7. 62 Melita St, Valletta ⓦ lafalconeria. com. An ultra-modern boutique with all the amenities of a large hotel, just on a smaller scale. The fitness centre, small indoor pool

Accommodation price codes

Throughout the guide, accommodation is categorized according to a price code, which roughly corresponds to the following price ranges. Price categories reflect the cost of a double room, with breakfast, in peak season.

€ = under €50
€€ = €50–150
€€€ = €150–250
€€€€ = over €250

(located in an alluring limestone cistern), rooftop terrace with city views, on-site café, restaurant and 24/7 reception ensure you'll want for nothing during your stay. €€€

LUCIANO AL PORTO BOUTIQUE MAP P.28, POCKET MAP E7. 255 St Ursula St, Valletta ☎ 7711 1110. Located atop the popular *Bridge Bar* (see page 37), *Luciano Al Porto Boutique* is easily recognized by its traditional bright red wooden balconies, which means it is perhaps the most photographed guesthouse in Valletta. Rooms are individually decorated with quirky local touches throughout; most offer Grand Harbour views. €€€

OSBORNE MAP P.28, POCKET MAP E7. 50 Triq Nofs In-Nhar, Valletta ⓦ osbornehotel. com. The *Osborne* offers a spot of British comfort and style in Valletta. A distinctly old-world atmosphere in the lobby gives way to 63 comfortably furnished rooms and a compact rooftop terrace and pool. €€

PALAZZO CONSIGLIA MAP P.28, POCKET MAP F7. 102 St Ursula St, Valletta ⓦ palazzoconsiglia.com. A thirteen-room boutique hotel with individually decorated rooms boasting hardwood floors and small lounges. The palazzo's former cellar is now a modern spa with an indoor pool. Two unusual features include a glass elevator in the palazzo's glass-roofed courtyard lobby and a little rooftop plunge pool that overlooks a crimson church dome. €€€

PHOENICIA MAP P.28, POCKET MAP D7. The Mall, Floriana ⓦ phoeniciamalta. com. Valletta's most deluxe hotel was constructed in the 1930s and has been beautifully upheld since; it is now tastefully decorated in a colonial-meets-Mediterranean style throughout. Facilities are extensive and impossibly elegant, including 7.5 acres of mature gardens and a luxurious infinity pool. This impressive hotel has played host to the likes of Queen Elizabeth II, Alec Guinness and Arnold Schwarzenegger. €€€€

THE SAINT JOHN MAP P.28, POCKET MAP F6. 176 Merchant St, Valletta ⓦ thesaintjohnmalta.com. A 21-room hotel with sleekly styled rooms encircling a sun-drenched interior courtyard. In each, mobile phones can be used to control room temperature and order room service. A stylish on-site gastro pub offers a selection of local beers (and garden swings as seating). €€€

SU29 BOUTIQUE HOTEL MAP P.28, POCKET MAP E7. 29 St Ursula Steps, Valletta ⓦ Su29hotel.com. This stylish boutique hotel might have come straight out of New York or London, offering a striking contrast between original features (wooden beams and exposed limestone walls) and trendy details (marble floors, glass walls). Its eight suites have orthopedic mattresses, original art and Dermalogica beauty products. €€

TANO'S BOUTIQUE GUESTHOUSE MAP P.28, POCKET MAP E7. 41 St Paul St, Valletta ⓦ tanosguesthouse.com. A pleasant, modern guesthouse set in a traditional townhouse with arched limestone ceilings, exposed wooden beams and original Maltese tiles. All rooms are individually decorated. €€€

TRITONI HARBOUR SUITES MAP P.28, POCKET MAP E7. 48 St Ursula St, Valletta

Author picks

Luxury: *Kempinski Resort* see page 134
Boutique: *Casa Ellul* see page 128
Traditional: *Luciano Al Porto Boutique* see page 128
Budget: *Inhawi Boutique Hostel* see page 131
Family: *DB San Antonio Hotel & Spa* see page 132

Ⓦ tritonharboursuitesvalletta.com.
Sleek, modern, self-catered apartments
with kitchenettes and sofa areas, plus a
shared terrace and charming furnished
courtyard. €€

The Three Cities

BOCO BOUTIQUE HOTEL MAP P.48,
POCKET MAP G9. 65 Oratory St, Cospicua
Ⓦ bocoboutique.com. A six-room boutique
hotel in a four-hundred-year-old Maltese
townhouse, located off the beaten path
in Cospicua. Rooms are designed by local
artists and charming details are abundant,
including upcycled furniture. €€

LOCANDA GELSOMINA MAP P.48,
POCKET MAP G9. 3 Popular Council St,
Birgu Ⓦ locandalagelsomina.com. Situated
in Birgu's Collachio, this pretty boutique
hotel is set in an early sixteenth-century
palazzo uniquely accented with Asian art
collected during the owner's travels. Four
suites are individually and luxuriously
decorated. Yoga retreats (2–7 days) and in-
house massages are also offered. Minimum
stay two nights. €€€

Sliema and St Julian's

115 THE STRAND SUITES MAP P.56,
POCKET MAP C5. The Strand, Sliema
Ⓦ 115thestrand.com. Located 100m away
from the Gżira seafront promenade, these
apartments are furnished in a comfortable
and modern style, with a/c, balconies,
kitchens and laundry facilities. €€

BARCELÓ FORTINA MAP P.56,
POCKET MAP A4. Tigné Seafront, Sliema
Ⓦ barcelo.com. Swanky five-star with a
prime location overlooking the waterfront
in upmarket Sliema. The rooms are
contemporary and tasteful in design and

supremely comfortable, all with terraces
and most overlooking the sea; there's an
indoor (guests-only) and outdoor (public)
pool, a huge state-of-the-art gym, and
stylish restaurant and bar. €€€

BOHO HOSTEL MAP P.56, POCKET MAP
A4. Villa Cycas, Dun G. Xerri St, St Julian's
Ⓦ bohohostel.com. *Boho Hostel* lives up to
its name, with eclectic style and rainbow-
coloured rooms. Its standout feature is the
lively garden, with multiple outdoor dining
areas, barbecue and hammocks. Shared
facilities include a lounge/TV area and
kitchen. €

CAVALIERI ART HOTEL MAP P.56,
POCKET MAP B2. Spinola Rd, St Julian's
Ⓦ cavalierihotel.com. There's nothing
particularly artistic about this hotel, but
it does offer comfortable and affordable
rooms, many with expansive views of
Spinola and Balluta Bays, plus an outdoor
pool that overlooks the sea. €€

CORINTHIA HOTEL ST GEORGE'S BAY
MAP P.56, POCKET MAP A1. St George's
Bay, St Julian's Ⓦ corinthia.com. The
five-star *Corinthia* is elegantly luxurious
with extensive facilities, including six
pools, a diving school, water sports and
sailing facilities, and a luxury spa. Rooms
are classically styled in warm ochre tones.
A courtesy bus transports guests to Sliema,
St Julian's, Valletta and the Royal Malta
Golf Club. Eight on-site restaurants offer a
range of tempting options from molecular
cuisine to English afternoon tea. €€€€

THE DISTRICT HOTEL MAP P.56, POCKET
MAP A1. Triq Santu Wistin, Paċeville.
com.mt. A chic option on the outskirts of
Paċeville. Although the *District* does not
have any facilities, it is considerably more
affordable than other hotels in the area. €€

THE GEORGE MAP P.56, POCKET MAP A1. Paċeville Ave, St Julian's ⓦ thegeorgemalta.com. Situated in the heart of Malta's clubbing district, with a suitably hip design and small rooftop pool. A bright, cheerful lobby leads to basic spa facilities. Rooms are spacious and tranquil. €€

HILTON MAP P.56, POCKET MAP B2 Portomaso, St Julian's ⓦ hilton.com. One of Malta's most sumptuous and glitzy hotels, with an elegant lobby awash in soft greys and twinkling silver chandeliers, plus sumptuously appointed rooms, all with balconies or terraces. The Hilton has three restaurants, four bars, four outdoor pools, a spa, fitness centre, tennis and squash courts, two children's pools and a heated indoor pool. With its crèche club services (fees apply), this is a popular hotel for families. €€€€

HOSTEL MALTI MAP P.56, POCKET MAP A3. 4 Birkirkara Hill, St Julian's ⓦ hostelmalti.org. Located in a converted townhouse, this hostel is a kaleidoscope of colour. Common areas include two shared kitchens, TV lounge and terrace with jacuzzi. Quiet time begins at 11pm but nightly pub-crawls are organized so you can mix and mingle off-site. €

HOTEL JULIANI MAP P.56, POCKET MAP A2. 25 St George's Rd, St Julian's.com. The Juliani's facade retains the look of a typical Baroque townhouse but the interior is refreshingly modern. 47 rooms, thirteen of which are suites, are each appointed with spacious bathrooms and large beds. Facilities include a small gym and luxurious rooftop lounge offering impressive views of Spinola Bay. Also home to the superb Asian fusion restaurant, Zest (see page 62). €€

HOTEL VALENTINA MAP P.56, POCKET MAP B2. Dobbie St, Paċeville, St Julian's ⓦ hotelvalentina.com. A refreshingly modern, 128-room hotel with a sleek lobby, bar and outdoor terraces at ground level. Staff are welcoming and helpful, and rooms are decorated in a minimal but comfortable style. A rooftop lap pool is open from April–Oct. The excellent Chalice Bar is located just across the street, and a 2min walk brings you to Malta's main restaurant district and the sea. €€

IKYK MAP P.56, POCKET MAP A1. 13 Wilga St, St Julian's ⓦ ikcollection.com. Those looking to stay in style on a budget could do worse than this vibrant, arty hotel, whose modern rooms are great value. There's burgers and pizzas at the on-site Bites, or pan-Asian food at Alu. €€

INHAWI BOUTIQUE HOSTEL MAP P.56, POCKET MAP B4. Hill St, Balluta Bay, St Julian's ⓦ inhawi.com. Overlooking one of the area's only green valleys, Malta's most luxurious hostel has beautiful Scandinavian-inspired interiors that are nicer than many hotels. Facilities include a communal kitchen, small garden with hammock, 24/7 reception and a large pool. €

INTERCONTINENTAL MALTA MAP P.56, POCKET MAP A1. St George's Bay, St Julian's. ⓦ malta.intercontinental. com. Located in the middle of Malta's clubbing district, the 480 rooms at the InterContinental are tastefully and luxuriously decorated. Facilities include a kids' club, fitness centre, squash courts, hair salon, business centre, lagoon-style outdoor swimming pool, heated indoor swimming pool, spa and glitzy rooftop infinity pool. "Luxury Highline Suites" include butler service, and all guests enjoy access to the nearby InterContinental Beach Club. €€€

MARCO POLO HOSTEL MAP P.56, POCKET MAP A2. Triq Ross, St Julian's ⓦ marcopolomalta.com. Self-styled as a "party hostel", this is a place for good times with new friends. To that end, there's a rooftop bar terrace and a full programme of activities, from pub crawls and barbecues to tours of the Blue Lagoon. When it's finally bedtime, choose between 6- or 12- bed dorms, or comfortable privates. €

ONYX HOTEL MAP P.56, POCKET MAP B2. 2 Ross St, Paċeville ⓦ onyxhotel.mt. Onyx Hotel, located in the heart of the clubbing district of Paċeville, offers well-appointed apartments with warm furnishings, kitchens, and large balconies, as well as hotel-styled rooms without self-catering facilities. €€

THE PALACE MAP P.56, POCKET MAP D4. High St, Sliema Ⓦ thepalacemalta.com. *The Palace* is part-boutique, part-large hotel, with distinctly themed suites, junior suites and modern rooms. Suites offer quirky details (think 1950s jukeboxes). There's also an on-site spa, fitness centre, indoor/outdoor pools and several good restaurants. Unlike most hotels in Sliema, it's situated in the village centre: a 5min walk brings you to the sea and Malta's main shopping district. €€€

PEBBLES BOUTIQUE APARTHOTEL MAP P.56, POCKET MAP C4. 88 The Strand, Sliema Ⓦ pebblessliema.com. mt. A modern seafront apart-hotel above a popular string of bars and restaurants. Apartments have a/c, kitchens and lounges. Superior apartments also have spacious sea-view terraces. Hotel-style amenities include 24hr reception, a rooftop terrace with jacuzzi, and free access to the nearby MedAsia lido (see page 58). €€€

THE VICTORIA HOTEL MAP P.56, POCKET MAP C4. Ġorġ Borg Olivier St, Sliema Ⓦ victoriahotel.com. As its name might suggest, *The Victoria Hotel* blends sleek Mediterranean and British style. Facilities include a compact gym and outdoor pool. A charming pub, *The Penny Black*, serves local lager by the pint alongside proper fish and chips. €€€

WESTIN MAP P.56, POCKET MAP B1. Dragonara Rd, St Julian's Ⓦ westinmalta. com. Situated on the coast at the outskirts of Paceville, this attractive pink building oozes old-school style and charm. Central but secluded, the *Westin* is an ideal base for exploring Malta while intermittently soaking up the sun at its indoor/outdoor pools or two private beaches. If you're visiting on the weekend, the lobby bar is an ideal spot for afternoon tea. A glitzy casino is located on site. €€€

Mdina and Rabat

POINT DE VUE MAP P.66. 2 Saqqajja Square, Rabat Ⓦ pointdevue-mdina.com.

A modest but comfortable fifteen-room guesthouse located on a public square-cum-car park just outside of Mdina's fortified walls. Several rooms at this seventeenth-century converted palazzo offer sweeping countryside views. On the ground floor, a busy family restaurant serves up rustic fare. €€

XARA PALACE RELAIS & CHATEAUX MAP P.66. Misrah Il-Kunsill Mdina Ⓦ xarapalace.com.mt. Set in a seventeenth-century palace, this intimate and impossibly romantic hotel is one of Malta's best (and a favourite of Hollywood celebrities). An elegant lobby is arranged around a central courtyard, with creeping ivy and a glass roof. Most rooms are duplexes with one-of-a-kind antiques, king-sized beds, and a full range of modern facilities. Those at the back have sweeping views of northern Malta, and some boast terraces with jacuzzis. An outdoor pool is located at the nearby Xara Lodge, a 5min drive away (courtesy shuttles provided). Two top-notch restaurants include the exquisite *De Mondion* (see page 73). €€€€

Central Malta

CORINTHIA PALACE HOTEL & SPA MAP P.76. De Paule Ave, San Anton, Balzan Ⓦ corinthia.com. Set across from the San Anton Gardens (see page 74) in the manicured suburbs of central Malta, this Grande Dame offers a pleasant respite from the chaos of Malta's main tourist areas. Rooms are classically decorated with a touch of intimacy and homeliness. Mature gardens provide a picturesque setting for two pools, four restaurants and a "Zen" spa. €€€

The north

DB SAN ANTONIO HOTEL & SPA MAP P.84, POCKET MAP G11. Tourist St, Qawra Ⓦ dbhotelsresorts.com. This all-inclusive resort is one of the largest in Malta, with five hundred rooms and suites. Its exterior is imposing and bland, but the huge range of facilities includes two outdoor pools, an adults-only rooftop pool and deck, a private sandy beach, a kids'/teens' area with animators, free dance

Rooms with a view

nd aqua sport classes, five restaurants, wo bars, a spa and gym. For such a arge resort, the rooms are surprisingly leasant, with a modern Moorish theme. an Antonio's sister hotel, the *DB Seabank Resort & Spa*, is located in nearby Mellieħa nd offers similar facilities, but rooms (same price) follow a nautical theme. Four ights minimum stay. €€€

DOUBLETREE BY HILTON MAP P.84, POCKET MAP G11. Dolmen St, Buġıbba Ⓦ dolmen.com.mt. Opening in 2024, this hotel has a range of modern facilities including four outdoor pools, a private beach and adjacent beach club, indoor pool, luxury spa, gym, and casino. Rooms are awash in fresh pine and are comfortably appointed; some have large terraces. €€€

MARITIM ANTONINE MAP P.89. Ġorġ Borg Olivier St, Mellieħa Ⓦ maritim. com.mt. An attractive cream-and-maroon building in Mellieħa's town centre, designed to look like a series of townhouses. Rooms lack a personal touch but are modern and spacious (some also have balconies). Facilities include a swimming pool in small but lush gardens, and an on-site spa. A rooftop restaurant offers stunning views of Mellieħa's parish church and Għadira beach. €€

PARK LANE APARTHOTEL MAP P.84, POCKET MAP G11 Maskli St, Qawra Ⓦ parklanemalta.com. The adults-only *Park Lane Aparthotel* offers self-catering apartments and studios. Rooms are bright and airy, with free wi-fi, sleek kitchenettes and a small dining area and lounge. There's also an outdoor pool. €€

QAWRA PALACE HOTEL MAP P.84. Dawret Il-Qawra, Qawra Ⓦ qawrapalacemalta.com. This hotel

offers ample facilities together with a comfortable, relaxed and friendly atmosphere. This is the perfect hotel for families and couples of all ages that are in search of a central location, with a good range of facilities close by. €€

RADISSON GOLDEN SANDS MAP P.80. Golden Bay, Mellieħa Ⓦ radissonblu. com. The five-star *Radisson Golden Sands* is the most luxurious in the north. The resort comprises 144 rooms and 164 suites furnished in a slightly bland but modern style. Four restaurants, a luxury spa, a private beach, pools, child-minding services and water sports mean you'll never have to leave the resort – and panoramic views of Golden Bay mean you may not want to. €€€€

SALINI RESORT MAP P.84, POCKET MAP H11. Salina Bay, St Paul's Bay Ⓦ saliniresort.com. This large resort boasts 237 bright and airy rooms, with a/c, TV and private balconies. Four restaurants, including a superb pizzeria, are located on site. Self-catering rooms with kitchenettes are also an option. Resort facilities include a luxury spa, fitness centre, indoor heated pool, tennis courts, and two outdoor pools, one of which is a palm-tree-lined infinity pool with expansive views of St Paul's Bay. €€

The south

DUNCAN GUESTHOUSE MAP P.100. 32 Xatt Is-Sajjieda, Marsaxlokk Ⓦ duncanguesthouse.com. Set adjacent to Marsaxlokk's parish church, this guesthouse has ten studio apartments. Although quite rustic, they are spacious with fridge, coffee machine, toaster, sink, a/c and TV. Some also have balconies overlooking Marsaxlokk's colourful harbour. €€

PORT VIEW GUESTHOUSE MAP P.100. Luzzu St, Marsaxlokk Ⓦ portviewmalta. com. A comfortable guesthouse with thirteen modern and spacious rooms, including quads for families. Breakfast is served on the rooftop terrace with harbour views. €€

QUAYSIDE APARTMENTS MAP P.100. 1 Fisherman's Wharf, Marsaxlokk Ⓦ quaysidemalta.com. Charming street-level apartments located in a converted nineteenth-century townhouse, with colourful front doors that match those of nearby fishing boats. Charming rustic features include exposed limestone walls, wooden ceiling beams and patterned Maltese floor tiles. Each apartment is equipped with TV, kitchenette, laundry facilities, living room and interconnecting bedrooms. Apartments share a common garden. €€

Gozo

B&B DAR TA' ZEPPI MAP P.104. 39 28th April 1688 St, Qala Ⓦ dartazeppi.com. A friendly Belgian artist and her Gozitan husband run this quaint five-room B&B. Rooms feature local art, colourful tiled floors and tall, wooden-beamed ceilings. Common facilities include a swimming pool, garden, and table tennis. Yoga, meditation and art workshops are also offered. €€

CASA GEMELLI MAP P.106. Republic St, Victoria Ⓦ tamariagozo.com. Beautiful Gozitan townhouse in a prime location in Victoria, with plush and classically decorated (if not slightly dated) rooms – think wooden ceiling beams, big brass beds, and lovely Maltese floor tiles. €€

THE DUKE BOUTIQUE HOTEL MAP P.106. Republic St, Victoria Ⓦ thedukehotelgozo. com. A modern boutique hotel located on the fourth and fifth floors of the Duke Shopping Complex, next to Victoria's pretty Villa Rundle Gardens (see page 105). Rooms, awash with marble, command views of the Citadel or have a private terrace with jacuzzi. Its location is unbeatable, with frequent transport links. €€

ELLIE BOO BED & BREAKFAST MAP P.108. 104 Ballura St, Xaghra Ⓦ bbgozo. com. Run by a British family, shared facilities at this homely B&B include an outdoor pool, lounge with TV and a hammock-slung garden with views of Gozo's verdant valleys. €€

GOZO ESCAPE MAP P.108. Various locations, Gozo Ⓦ gozoescape.com. These fourteen beautiful farmhouses located throughout Gozo each sleep a minimum of four. Most are over three-hundred years old and all have outdoor pools, a/c and wood-burning fireplaces. Seven nights minimum stay in July/August. €€

GRAND HOTEL MAP P.104. Sant Antnin St, Mġarr Ⓦ grandhotelmalta. com. An imposing hybrid of Baroque and Neoclassical design overlooking Mġarr harbour. Rooms are comfortably furnished in a classic style and have a/c and TVs. A large range of facilities including cinemas, a games room, a basic gym and an outdoor swimming pool with impressive views. €€

KEMPINSKI SAN LAWRENZ RESORT MAP P.114. Rokon St, San Lawrenz Ⓦ kempinski.com. Gozo's most luxurious resort, and undoubtedly one of the country's best. The lobby boasts coffered wooden ceilings and superb contemporary art, while the best of the rooms have sizeable terraces from which you can see Dwejra's bright green terraced fields just beyond the hotel's grounds. Mature gardens are a major draw – fragrant flowers, palm trees and water features surround three spotlessly clean pools, and vegetable allotments provide fresh ingredients for three top-notch restaurants and an impressive breakfast buffet. The hotel's luxury spa offers two indoor pools, steam chamber and Ayurvedic treatments. Courtesy shuttles offer easy access to top sites. €€€€

MARIA GIOVANNA GUEST HOUSE MAP P.108. Rabat Road, Marsalforn Ⓦ tamariagozo.com. Lying a 2min walk from Marsalforn beach, this fifteen-room guesthouse offers double rooms (some with sea views) in a typically rustic Gozitan style with pine furniture, wrought-iron beds and quirky bric-a-brac. €€

URELLA LIVING B&B MAP P.108. 18
ven St, Marsalforn ⓦ murellaliving.com.
t. The best value for money in Marsalforn,
is colourful, ultra-modern B&B feels
ery much like a boutique hotel, with large
esigner rooms. €€

UAINT HOTELS MAP P.104. 13
ecember St, Nadur ⓦ quainthotelsgozo.
om. Twelve spacious, ultra-modern rooms
ncluding three penthouses) in the heart
f Nadur village life. A second location in
ewkija (ten rooms) is equally pleasant. €€

A ĊENĊ MAP P.104. Ċenċ St, Ta Sannat
Ⓦ vjborg.com. Once a grand five-star
otel attracting Hollywood celebrities, the
ld-world-style *Ta Ċenċ* offers a pleasantly
ecluded atmosphere and an extensive
rray of facilities, including indoor/outdoor
wimming pools, tennis courts, and a
rivate beach at the magnificent Mġarr

Ix-Xini (see page 109). Guest rooms are
housed in stone bungalows with private
terraces or gardens. Courtesy shuttles
service main sites. Three nights minimum
stay in high season. €€€€

TOWNHOUSE 17 MAP P.106. Triq Taħt
Putirjal, Victoria ⓦ townhouse17.com.
Right in the heart of things in Victoria,
this modern hotel combines an intimate
atmosphere with contemporary design.
There are just nine guestrooms, with
panelled pine walls and minimalist
decor which contrasts nicely with the
historic setting of the house itself and
its surroundings, evident as you open
your French windows and step onto your
balcony. Unusually, single rooms are also
available for solo travellers. The *Bistro
Chapeau* downstairs is a friendly spot,
open all day for filling and good-value
grub. €€

ESSENTIALS

Carnival

Arrival

International flights arrive at Malta International Airport, around 8km (20min drive) south of Valletta. There's a **taxi stand** at the arrivals terminal; a list of standard fares is posted and fares are paid in advance at the designated ticket counter. Better value are the taxi apps, with Bolt the most widespread, and Uber also available. Public **buses** stop just outside the departures terminal and service all regions frequently. There's also a direct bus (X1; 1hr journey) to the Gozo **ferry** at Ċirkewwa. For detailed bus schedules visit the Malta Public Transport kiosk in the arrivals hall.

Getting around

By bus

With an extensive and cheap network of **buses**, it's relatively easy to explore Malta and Gozo via public transport. Malta's fleet of public buses are modern and air-conditioned and call at three main hubs: Valletta, Sliema, the airport in Luqa, and the ferry terminal at Ċirkewwa. Services start at 5.30am and run until 11pm; there's also a night bus service on Fridays and Saturdays departing from Paċeville, the main clubbing district. During the summer months, an extra night bus service departs Ta Qali, where Malta's major outdoor clubs are located. Night bus services cost €3 per trip. Buses are numbered and full **route maps and schedules** can be found on ⓦ publictransport.com.mt, on the free Tallinja app, and on Google Maps. Hard copies of bus schedules and maps of bus routes are also available from tourist offices and bus stations.

Bus tickets can be purchased in cash from your bus driver, or at a sales and information office, which are located at the Valletta bus terminal, Sliema ferries terminal, Malta International Airport, Mater Dei hospital, Buġibba bus terminal and Victoria bus terminal. **Bus passes** called "Explore Cards" for unlimited travel are sold at the bus stations; they're valid for seven days, including two trips on the Valletta-Sliema–Birgu ferry services and a hop-on hop-off bus tour or boat trip to Comino. You can also purchase a block of twelve one-day travel tickets; these can be used yearlong.

Most buses are equipped with an automated audio system to announce upcoming stops. If you're in doubt, drivers are normally happy to tell you where to get off.

By car

The downsides of **renting a car**, aside from the expense, are the poor road conditions in rural areas and the chaotic local driving habits. To rent a car or a motorbike, you'll need to present a valid driving licence, and you must be over 21. You may also need to show your passport, and some firms ask for a cash deposit or credit card imprint. An optional extra charge for comprehensive insurance cover is worthwhile considering Malta's high accident rates; otherwise, damage to the vehicle can incur a hefty insurance excess. Average rates for a four-door car are usually discounted if you rent for longer than five days (local companies typically offer cheaper rates than international brands). All of the following companies can arrange for cars to be picked up and left at the airport or other locations, and in all cases you can get a quote, book and pay via their website: **Aquarius Rent A Car** (117 St Paul's Street, St Paul's Bay Ⓦ aquariusrentacar.com); **Budget** (50 Msida Seafront, Msida Ⓦ budget.com.mt); **Thrifty** (Malta International Airport Arrivals lounge Ⓦ thrifty.com); **Mirage** (246 Tourist Road, Bugibba Ⓦ miragecarhire.com); **Hertz** (Malta International Airport Ⓦ hertz.com.mt); **Mayjo Car Rentals** (Triq Fortunato Mizzi, Rabat, Gozo Ⓦ mayjocarhire.com); **Rabat Garage** (92 Triq Kola Xagħra, Rabat Ⓦ rabatgarage.com); **Sixt** (Malta International Airport Arrivals lounge Ⓦ sixt.com).

By scooter, quad bike or bicycle

To rent a **scooter**, the minimum age requirement is 18–23 (depending on company and bike size). Drivers must hold a driving licence (most rental scooters in Malta are 125cc), and most companies require a refundable security deposit. If you rent a scooter, bear in mind that bends can be slippery (because of dust/oil build-up). Watch out for potholes and wear a helmet (usually provided by the rental company). **Quad bikes** are particularly popular in Gozo. Gozo Quad Hire (Borg Għarib St, Għajnsielem, Gozo Ⓦ gozoquadhire.com) offers them per day or for two days or more (drivers must be 21 or older). In Malta, Tony's Rentals (46 The Strand, Sliema Ⓦ carrentalmalta.eu) also offers quads. Alternatively, try AHS Malta (200 San Albert St, Gżira Ⓦ ahsmalta.com).

Ecobikes Malta (8 Imsel St, Bugibba Ⓦ bikerentalmalta.com) offers **mountain bike** and e-bike rentals against a deposit. For beginners, Gozo Adventures (7 Saint Indrija St, Victoria, Gozo Ⓦ gozoadventures.com) also offers guided **bicycle tours** (including guide and lunch). Most reputable providers offer helmets, locks and repair kits at no extra charge. Although the rural areas of Gozo and Malta can be pleasant to explore by bike, and distances are short, the topography is hilly and the summer heat can be exhausting. If you're interested in renting a bicycle for transport within and between villages, **Next Bike** (charged by the minute or the day; Ⓦ nextbike.com.mt) is a good option. Malta's national bicycle rental service has self-service terminals across the island at major tourist centres (Valletta, Sliema, St Julian's). You can register at any terminal or on the Next Bike app, which provides a code to unlock your bicycle. Bikes can be returned at any terminal in the network. Bear in mind motorists are still growing accustomed to sharing the road with cyclists – exercise extreme caution and stick to the seafront to avoid exhausting hills. Also note that helmets are not provided with Next Bikes. Other reputable bike rental outlets include Eco Sports Ltd (8 Triq L-Imsell, St Paul's Bay Ⓦ ecosportsltd.com) and The Cyclist (Rihan St, San Gwann Ⓦ thecyclistmalta.com).

By taxi

Official **taxis** are white and have their registration number painted on the side of the car. There are plenty of strategically located **taxi stands** in the central areas, with main stands at the airport, Valletta bus terminal, Bisazza Street Sliema, Bugibba. Though taxis have meters, they're rarely used, and fares are often arbitrary – in most cases, drivers will try to squeeze as much money out of you as possible (for a stomach-rolling ride, to boot). The airport is the only place where white taxi fares are fixed and strictly enforced. After the buses have stopped running at about 11pm, taxi prices generally go up by about a third. Several companies offer a slightly more expensive but considerably more comfortable 24hr service with free wi-fi and SMS notifications – good options include eCabs (☎ 2138 3838 ⓦ ecabs.com. mt) and Hello Cabs (☎ 9903 4133 ⓦ hellocabsmalta.com). Haggling isn't necessary with these operators; you'll be quoted a fixed fare online or by phone. In Gozo you'll find white taxis at Mġarr Harbour and in Victoria at the bus station and Independence Square, but at night you won't find taxis anywhere and you would have to pre-arrange with a chauffeur-driven service – try Mayjo in Rabat (☎ 2155 6678 or ☎ 2155 1772). The shortcomings of the traditional taxi companies mean that the best option is to use a taxi app – Bolt is the most popular, followed by Uber. Both operate across Malta and Gozo, and will even pick up in smaller towns and rural areas; in the cities they will be there at a moment's notice. The apps are also generally cheaper than the traditional taxis.

Directory A–Z

Accessible travel

Planning rules have only had to make provision for people with disabilities in the last decade, and facilities generally remain rather poor. Many upmarket hotels have specially equipped rooms and most public buses can accommodate wheelchairs. Johns company offers wheelchair-friendly taxis (ⓦ johns.com.mt). The National Commission for Persons with Disabilities (Psaila Street, Birkirkara ⓦ crpd.org.mt) is focused on fostering a national framework for people with disabilities, not providing general information, though you can contact them if you're stuck or need any information and assistance.

Addresses

House and building numbers are uncommon in Malta. Houses and buildings are typically referred to by names (e.g. "Santa Marija" house) or simply by their street name or nearby landmarks. To confuse matters further, English and Maltese street names are used interchangeably (for example, Triq and Street). To inform a taxi driver of your destination, a street name and village name (or, even better, just a hotel name) is usually sufficient. The correct mailing address format in Malta is: [Number] [Street Name] [Village] [Postcode]. Postcodes can be found online at ⓦ maltapost.com/postcodes.

Cinema

All mainstream cinemas have modern theatres and generally feature Hollywood releases. Options include the two-screen Citadel Cinema (13 It-Telgħa tal-Belt, Victoria, Gozo ⓦ citadelcinema.com); the thirteen-screen Eden Century Cinemas (St George's Bay, St Julian's ⓦ edencinemas.com.mt); the six-screen Embassy (Saint Lucy Street, Valletta ⓦ embassycinemas.com); and the Galleria Cinema Fgura (Zabbar Road, Fgura ⓦ galleria.com.mt).

Crime

Malta has a very low crime rate and remains one of those rare places where many locals don't even lock their front doors. Even in busy tourist areas, pickpocketing and theft are not very common. Exercise common sense while exploring (lock your car doors, mind your luggage, protect your passport) but you needn't wear a money belt or wear your backpack on your front. Walking alone at night is safe in nearly all areas, and CCTV is in use in public spaces.

Emergencies

For police, ambulance and fire services, call ☎ 112; for air rescue call ☎ 2124 4371 (☎ 2182 4220 outside office hours, including weekends); for sea rescue call ☎ 2123 8797. If you're involved in a traffic accident call Local Wardens on ☎ 2132 0202.

Electricity
The supply is 240V; plugs are three-pin.

Embassies and consulates
UK High Commission (Whitehall Mansions, Ta Xbiex Seafront ☎ 2323 0000); US Embassy (Ta Qali National Park, Attard ☎ 2561 4000); Canada Consulate (Demajo House, 103 Archbishop St, Valletta ☎ 2552 3233); Australia High Commission (Ta' Xbiex Terrace, Ta' Xbiex ☎ 2133 0201).

Health
Hospitals: Mater Dei (University Heights, Msida ☎ 2545 000); Gozo General Hospital (Victoria, Gozo ☎ 2156 6000).

Internet
Free wi-fi is available in public squares and gardens (look for the MCA free network).

Laundry
There are a handful of strategically located laundries, some with coin-operated machines. Malta's largest company, Portughes, has four main outlets and five pick up/drop off points within stationery shops and convenience stores, including one in Sannat, Gozo; they do pick-ups and deliveries from any address (⊕ portughes.com).

Left luggage
Most hotels in Malta offer free luggage storage. You can also store luggage at the Malta International Airport's Departures Hall (open 24/7 – presentation of valid ID is required and valuable items, such as personal electronics, are not accepted).

LGBTQ+ travellers
Over the last few years, Malta has experienced a definite and positive shift towards greater acceptance of the LGBTQ+ community in all aspects of life. It is a very safe destination for LGBTQ+ travellers and number one on the European Rainbow Index for eight consecutive years. Gay Guide Malta (⊕ gayguidemalta.com) offers a wealth of information on events, LGBTQ+ friendly accommodation and the best entertainment venues. LGBTQ+ friendly bars and clubs include *S2S Events* (Gianpula Road, Rabat); *Michelangelo Club Lounge* (St Rita's Steps, Paceville); *The Birdcage Lounge* (Triq il-Kbira, Rabat); *Q-bar* (Valletta Waterfront, Valletta); and *Bridge Bar* (Liesse, Valletta).

Lost property
You can reclaim lost property at the **Malta International Airport** (where it's held for 30 days) at its main Customer Service desk. Lost property (especially wallets) is frequently turned in to police, so it's worth contacting the station. To report other lost property or a suspected theft, visit a Police Station or call ☎ 2122 4001. You can also file police reports online for lost property valued at less than €250 at ⊕ policereport.gov.mt.

Money
Malta's **currency** is the euro. Most **banks** open Mon–Fri from 8.30am–1.30pm and until midday on Sat; in towns, you'll never be

Eating price codes

Throughout the guide, restaurants, bars and nightclubs are categorized according to a price code, which roughly corresponds to the following price ranges. Price categories reflect the cost of a two-course meal, including an alcoholic drink, per person.

€ = under €15
€€ = €15–25
€€€ = €25–50
€€€€ = over €50

more than a ten-minute walk from one, and all branches have ATMs (in Gozo, however, there are only ATMs in Victoria, Nadur, Mġarr and Marsalforn). Banks offer the best rates for cash or travellers' cheques; exchange bureaux normally charge a higher commission of about three percent, though their opening hours tend to be more convenient, while hotels charge a similar commission and round off the exchange rate to their advantage. All major credit cards – Visa, Mastercard, American Express, Diners, as well as others – are widely accepted by shops, hotels, guesthouses and car rental companies, but it's best to carry some cash as smaller restaurants and cafés may not accept cards.

The **cost** of living and visiting Malta is rising. Supermarket prices reach EU averages, and restaurant prices are also rising; alcoholic drinks, however, are cheaper than in most European countries. Public transport is affordable, and entry fees for sights and museums are generally between €5–€10 (a Heritage Malta multi-site pass offers access to all 22 museums and sites). Accommodation will be your biggest expense (see page 128).

Opening hours

High street shops in Malta are generally open **Mon–Sat 9am–7pm**. Small or family-run shops usually close between 1pm and 4pm Mon–Fri, and at 1pm on Saturday. Almost all shops and supermarkets in Malta are closed on Sundays, with the exception of Arkadia supermarket (Portomaso Complex, St Julian's; Sun 8am–10pm), Scotts supermarket (Triq Amery, Sliema; Sun 8.30am–12.30pm) and Bay Street shopping complex (open daily 10am–10pm). Restaurants are open from 7pm for dinner Mon–Sat, and from noon to 3pm for lunch daily. Museums and galleries are generally open daily 10am–5pm, with last admissions from 4.30pm.

Pharmacies

The islands' many **pharmacies** open Mon–Sat 9am–7pm and some may take a break from 1.30pm–3pm. Daily newspapers and Ⓦ pharmacy.com.mt list those that open, on a roster basis, during evenings, Sundays and public holidays until 10pm. Pharmacies sell over-the-counter medicines, contact lenses and emergency contraception.

Phones

The **international dialling code** for Malta is +356. To avoid roaming charges, contact your mobile phone provider to check the rates and enquire about any available discounts. You can also purchase an eSIM to connect to the local network and download data packs without the hassle of obtaining a physical SIM card. This can also be done before setting off on your travels.

ost

here's a **post office** in virtually every town on the islands, most open Mon–Sat 7.30am–1pm although times may vary. Some post offices stay open until 3pm while others take a break at lunchtime and reopen from 4pm–6pm. International mail is dispatched on the next working day; to the UK it takes three to five business days; seven to ten business days to North America; and up to two weeks for Australia and New Zealand, although expected delivery times may vary.

Smoking

Smoking in public places is banned, but this is very loosely enforced. There's even smoking inside some night clubs. Cigarettes can be purchased from vending machines, located in most bars and some cafés.

Theatre

There are four theatres in the Maltese Islands and the season runs between Oct and May. Check at tourist offices for details of upcoming events, or keep an eye out for posters, as well as listings on theatre websites. Offerings are fairly varied, from mainstream touring productions to plays by Maltese companies, while theatres are also used to stage classical music concerts, opera and ballet. The **Astra Theatre** (9 Republic St, Victoria, Gozo ⓦ teatruastra.org. mt) is Malta's largest Baroque theatre and features anything from operas to drama and ballet. The large **Aurora Opera Theatre** (100 Republic St, Victoria, Gozo ⓦ teatruaurora.com) is renowned for excellent operas; it also stages drama and other events such as ballet. The eighteenth-century **Manoel Theatre** (115 Old Theatre St, Valletta ⓦ teatrumanoel.mt) is Malta's national theatre, and features drama and concerts. **Theatre in the Round** (St James Cavalier, Pope Pius 5 St, Valletta ⓦ kreattivita.org) is a small theatre with sixty seats arranged around the central stage.

Time

Malta is **one hour ahead of GMT** and observes daylight saving time.

Tipping

Locals round up to the nearest euro on a small bill or leave a 5–10 percent gratuity for a larger group. Tourists are expected to tip more (around 10 percent, you can leave it on the table). Tipping is not strictly required for taxi drivers or tour operators and is usually only used to reward excellent service. Tipping (a few euro) is expected for valets and waitors.

Tourist information

Local and overseas offices of the Malta Tourism Authority supply leaflets on sights and activities, as well as free maps and an annual calendar of events; staff can help with basic queries, and all local offices have lists of accommodation options. In some offices (such as at the airport), they can help you book accommodation on the spot. There are offices in the following places: Airport Arrivals Hall (ⓣ 2369 6073); Valletta 18, Valletta (ⓣ 2291 5504); 17 Independence Square, Rabat, Gozo (ⓣ 2291 5752); Birgu Inquisitor's Palace (Main Gate Street ⓣ 2291 5509);

Public holidays

Malta has fourteen public holidays: Jan 1, Feb 10, March 19, Good Friday, March 31, May 1, June 7, June 29, Aug 15, Sept 8, Sept 21, Dec 8, Dec 13 and Dec 25.

Marsaxlokk (Xatt is-Sajjieda ☎ 9909 5698); Mdina (St Publius Square ☎ 9943 9867); Mellieħa (Misraħ iz-Zjara tal-Papa Ġwanni Pawlu II ☎ 2291 5511); Buġibba (Islets Promenade ☎ 2141 9176).

The Malta Tourism Authority's **website** for Gozo, ⓦ visitgozo.com, provides an overview of all major sites, attractions and activities, and a calendar of events. Malta Tourism Authority's website, ⓦ visitmalta.com, provides useful practical information and a calendar of events.

Travelling with children

Malta is a child-friendly destination, but it can be tricky to manoeuvre pram on the narrow streets of most villages. Sliema and St Julian's are the best bases for families, with their extensive promenades and newer and larger playgrounds at ix-Xatt ta' Qui-Si-Sana (near the main shopping district), Independence Gardens (also called Exiles, on Triq it Torri) and in Pembroke (Triq G. Portainer). Most public museums are free for children, while private attractions offer discounts.

Sports and outdoor activities

Watersports

Watersports outfits operate on many of the islands' main beaches between May and Oct, and offer everything from parasailing, waterskiing or wakeboarding, paddle boarding, jet-skiing, banana rides or jet pack hoverboarding to canoes and kayaks. Many also have self-driving speedboats for rent (no licence required). Reputable watersport companies include Sun & Fun (Corinthia Beach Resort, St George's Bay; ⓦ sunfunmalta.com) and Oh Yeah Sports (Tunny Net Complex, Mellieħa; ⓦ ohyeahmalta.com).

Snorkelling

With some of the clearest water in the Mediterranean, shallow and glass-calm in the summer, Malta boasts some superb snorkelling. A large concentration of marine life can be found in the nooks and crannies along the entirety of the islands' rocky shores. Underwater rocks harbour clusters of spiny sea urchins, inquisitive common octopus and beautiful red starfish. Finger-sized fishes such as blennies, grey triggerfish and Connemara suckerfish float in shallow waters, darting away as you get close to explore their variegated colours. Large, silvery

shoals of fish are also commonly seen close to the shoreline – these include bream, mullet, silverfish, sand smelt, chromis and wrasse. Recommended and conveniently situated snorkelling hotspots include the Exiles area in Sliema, and Golden Bay and Għajn Tuffieħa beaches. Further afield, Għar Lapsi and Mġarr ix-Xini (Gozo) are sure bets — but just about anywhere you take a dip in Malta you're likely to find the fish plentiful and the snorkelling satisfying.

Scuba diving

Malta's waters offer some of the best scuba diving in the Mediterranean and attract some 50,000 enthusiasts annually. Aside from stunning seascapes (from boulder meadows, to wartime wrecks, gulleys, labyrinthine caves, chimneys and ledges to sheer cliff-drops), underwater visibility is excellent here – 20m in spring and autumn during plankton build-up, and up to 45m between Nov and March – while the mild weather allows year-round diving (water temperatures rise to a peak average of 27°C in summer, and go down to just 15°C in winter). Shore and boat dive sites are scattered across the archipelago, but f the three islands, Gozo offers the most spectacular dive sites, especially ff Dwejra at the western tip (the Blue ole in Dwejra made it onto Jacques ousteau's top 10 worldwide). The asic rule of thumb is that the further orth you go, the better the diving.

The diving centres scattered roughout the islands are professional utfits affiliated with the major ternational schools (PADI, CMAS, SAC, SSI Advanced Open Water, etc) nd offer all the standard courses plus pecialized programmes such as night- cave-diving, as well equipment entals. Five-day open water courses nd advanced open water courses are n offer alongside shorter trips. Most chools also offer taster dives for he uninitiated – instructors take you own to a depth of up to 10m without he need of prior instruction. You can oin the diving centres in escorted or roup dives (including equipment), or, f you're a qualified diver, you can rent quipment and dive independently. n this case, bear in mind that some ives can be tricky for those not used o local conditions; fatal incidents are eported yearly in caves off Dwejra in iozo, when silt stirs up and obscures he caves' mouths.

Diving centres

MALTA
7R Diving St Julian's Aquatic Sports Club, George Borg Olivier St, St Julian's ⓦ 7rdiving.com.
Dive Systems Tower Point, Tower Rd, Sliema ⓦ divesystemsmalta.com.
Dive Wise Westin Dragonara Complex, St Julian's ⓦ divewise.com.mt.
Go Dive Malta 2 Triq Dun Grangisk Sciberras, Mellieħa ⓦ godivemalta.co.uk.
Maltaqua Mosta Rd, St Paul's Bay ⓦ maltaqua.com.

GOZO
Calypso Diving Centre Triq Marina, Marsalforn Bay Seafront

ⓦ calypsodivers.com.
Gozo Aqua Sports Rabat Rd, Marsalforn ⓦ gozoaquasports.com.
Ritual Xlendi Bay, 2/4 Triq il-Gostra ⓦ ritualdive.com.
Scuba Kings Dive Centre 46 Santa Maria St, Marsalforn ⓦ divemalta-gozo.com.

Hiking

The network of paths that criss-cross the Maltese countryside offer ample opportunity for hiking. We've detailed some short, scenic walks in the guide, but for longer hikes, head to Malta's south coast between Dingli Cliffs and Ras Il-Qammiegħ, or to Gozo's coastal cliffs between Mġarr Ix-Xini and Xlendi, Xlendi and Ras Il-Wardija, and San Blas Bay and Marsalforn. Visit Malta offers excellent, detailed and free walking guides with maps for these and other routes in English, French and German (ⓦ visitmalta.com).

The best time for hiking in Malta is winter (Oct–May), when the weather is mild and the landscape green. In summer, you'll find that only early morning or evening walking is comfortable (or, indeed, safe) and the parched countryside isn't that appealing. Bear in mind that during autumn and spring (and particularly in April and May), bird-hunters can be a nuisance; besides shattering the peace with shotgun blasts, hunters can get tetchy with strollers, largely because they are aware that non-hunters may disapprove. Although incidents are rare, if you encounter a hunter the most prudent thing to do is to greet him affably and keep going. It's also good to note that it's not always clear what land in the countryside is public or private, and even public access roads are frequently cordoned off with makeshift (illegal) signs or gates. The Tourism Information Office provides excellent guidance on accessible routes, as do local hiking groups. You can join the

Ramblers Association (@ramblersmalta.org) on one of its free walks for hikers of all levels between October and May (detailed programmes of walks are on the website). Another possibility is to walk with MC Adventures (@mcadventure.com.mt) who organize private, tailor-made walks.

Festivals and events

Carnival

Staged during the week preceding Lent, Valletta and Floriana's carnival parades feature large neon-coloured floats and professional dance troupes that compete for awards. Nadur in Gozo sees pre-Lenten celebrations that are closer to the mock-revolutionary origins of carnival, in which the underprivileged classes romped through the streets in an unruly display. Although modern influences are evident (you'll see lots of latex Halloween-style masks), the unorganized street theatre and performances are still driven by the original spirit, and many of the costumes are farcical parodies of the powers-that-be. Be aware that the scenes (and costumes) in Nadur can get bawdy and rowdy. Carnival weekend is one of the busiest times of the year in Gozo; unless you book months in advance you're unlikely to find accommodation, and ferry queues can be lengthy.

Easter

Each Good Friday, many Maltese towns stage sober biblical re-enactments. Starting at dusk, these impressive parades feature Biblical characters and statues representing the Stations of the Cross. Participants dress in white robes and hoods, and drag bundles of metal chains or wooden crosses, in penitence and holy self-mortification. The best re-enactments are held in Xagħra (see page 112), Żejtun (see page 98) and Valletta (see page 26). On Easter Sunday, towns all over Malta erupt in celebration, and events include sprinting with the statue of the Risen Christ to symbolize Christ's Resurrection – the most raucous event are held in Birgu (see page 46) and Xagħra after morning Mass at around 10am. Easter marks the beginning of high season tourism on the islands.

International Fireworks Festival

April @maltafireworksfestival.com
Usually hosted during the last week of April in Gozo and Malta, the International Fireworks Festival sees fireworks producers compete against each other with elaborate pyro-musical displays. Shows are always free and locations change every year, but typically the festival ends in a grand finale over the Grand Harbour in Valletta (best viewed from St Barbara's Bastions or Barriera Wharf).

Malta Music Week

June @isleofmtv.com
The last week of June is dedicated to clubbing in Malta with the Isle of MTV Malta Music Week bringing in top international acts for performances at Malta's largest open-air clubs. The week culminates in a huge free concert in Floriana.

Għanafest

June @festivals.mt
This two-day folk music festival takes place every year in June in different public gardens throughout Malta. The festival takes its name from Għana, a form of traditional Maltese folk singing.

Malta Jazz Festival

July @festivals.mt/mjf

alta's annual three-day jazz festival osted in mid-July at beautiful arrier Wharf, Valletta. For over ten ears, the Grand Harbour has offered n atmospheric backdrop for local nd foreign acts including Diana rall, Natalie Cole, Chick Corea, ayne Shorter and Mike Stern. Most vents are ticketed, but if you're nly interested in a casual look, erformances can be clearly heard and een from atop St Barbara's Bastions.

Vine festivals

uly and August ⓦ delicata.com,
ⓦ marsovinwinefestival.com

ach summer, Valletta hosts two wine estivals from local producers Marsovin July) and Delicata (August). The larsovin Festival is held at Hasting's ardens over three nights and offers he biggest venue with the best wines. ntrance is free and you pay for drink okens. The Delicata Wine Festival is osted later in the summer at Upper arrakka Garden, a smaller (more rowded) venue with superb views. This vent is all-you-can-drink for the price f a commemorative wine glass.

Notte Bianca

October ⓦ festivals.mt/nb

Like other White Nights across Europe, Valletta's Notte Bianca is a nocturnal contemporary arts festival. Typically hosted on the first Saturday of October or the last Saturday of September, it sees over a hundred free artistic and musical performances unfold across Valletta. The official programme of events is usually announced a month in advance.

Birgufest

October

This celebration of Birgu's beauty, history and culture is one of Malta's top annual events, hosted during the first weekend of October. The festival sees the village lit by hundreds of thousands of candles, often at their most abundant in the front parlours of Birgu's townhouses, where they are tucked into heaps of religious bric-a-brac. Front doors are thrown wide open for the public to enjoy the spectacle; a reminder of the warm hospitality (and low crime rates) on the island.

Malta Classic

October ⓦ maltaclassic.com

The Malta Classic is a four-day celebration of vintage style and classic cars hosted every October in Mdina. Local car collectors (of which there are a surprising number for such a small island) compete to win races in various categories. For tourists, the main draw of the event is the Concours d'Elegance, usually hosted on the Friday, which sees collectors in period dress showcasing their automotive gems in the village's picturesque square.

Christmas

December

From December 8th (a public holiday) onwards, locals start heading to Valletta to take in the beautiful light displays, do their Christmas shopping and enjoy a glass of mulled wine. Many parishes, as well as individuals, put up impressive mechanized cribs (called *presepju* in Maltese). In the weeks leading up to the big event, the entire Gozitan village of Ghajnsielem is transformed into an immersive re-enactment of Bethlehem, complete with dozens of volunteer actors playing the essential roles in the Christmas story. The religious build-up climaxes on Christmas Eve when most Maltese attend a ritualized version of High Mass at midnight, after which many families have a 2am "Christmas breakfast". On Christmas Day, families celebrate with elaborate multi-course meals including soup, lasagna, pasta, turkey and heaps of dessert and wine.

Chronology

c. 5000 BCE Neolithic people arrive in Malta from Sicily.

3600 BCE The first of the Neolithic temples – among the oldest extant buildings in the world – is constructed at Ġgantija, Gozo.

3300 BCE The Hypogeum of Ħal-Saflieni is constructed in present-day Tarxien, followed by the Tarxien Temple complex.

2500 BCE The Neolithic period comes to an inexplicable end.

2000 BCE Bronze-Age settlers inhabit Malta, erecting fortified castles and granaries on ridges and hills.

800–480 BCE The Phoenicians turn the island into a centre for sea trade. Mdina is established as Malta's first town and is to remain the capital for a millennium.

480 BCE–218 CE Malta falls under the control of Carthage.

60 Christian tradition holds that St Paul is shipwrecked in Malta on the way to his trial in Rome, and the first seeds of Christianity on the island are sown.

218 After several wars between Carthage and Rome, the latter finally consolidates its rule in Malta.

395–870 After the split in the Roman Empire, Malta falls under Byzantine rule.

870 Aghlabid Arabs coming from North Africa capture Malta, and Islamic rule begins – a period whose lasting legacy is the development of the Maltese language, architecture and irrigation systems that are still practised today, besides the introduction of orange and lemon trees.

1090–1530 Malta swings under the influence of a dizzying number of various rulers, including the Normans, Aragonese, Swabians and Angevins, as well as various regional strongmen and merchants who run the islands as their private fiefdom.

1530 Charles V of Spain gives Malta to the Knights of St John (now the Knights of Malta) in return for a Maltese falcon every year. The Knights, in retreat after being routed out of Rhodes by the Ottomans in 1522, put Malta on the frontline of the Muslim–Christian struggle for supremacy and territory. They establish their base in Birgu.

1551 Dragut Rias, an Ottoman general, attacks Malta with his fleet. The Knights repel the attack, and Dragut raids Gozo instead; he breaches the Ċittadella and almost the entire population is taken as slaves.

1565 Dragut leads a second attack with a massive show of force, but after his death and a war of attrition lasting six months, the Ottoman army is defeated in what's now known as the Great Siege of 1565.

1566 Work begins on Valletta, Malta's new fortified capital city.

1570 The Knights relocate their base to Valletta and begin construction on the city's most glorious auberges, palazzos and St John's Co-Cathedral. Their rule on the islands persists for two more centuries.

1798 Aided by treacherous Knights, Napoleon Bonaparte takes Malta in three days of light skirmishes; the Knights are forced to leave and Napoleon loots most of their riches to pay for his wars. Napoleon is in Malta for six days, during which time he abolishes feudal rights and slavery, establishes a Government Commission, public finance administration and the foundations for today's public judicial and education systems. Three months after the arrival of the French, the deeply Catholic Maltese revolt as the French have been closing convents and seizing church treasures. French forces retreat to Valletta, and the Maltese insurgents – aided by the British Army – lay siege; it takes two years before the starving French soldiers surrender.

1800 The British take possession of the islands.

1835 Britain rules the islands as a colony and sets up a Maltese Council of Government that advises the British governor.

World War I Britain turns Malta into the "Nurse of the Mediterranean", a centre for recuperating injured soldiers.

1919 Protests for greater autonomy from the British turn violent (British troops fire into a crowd, killing four). Britain moves fast to defuse the tension, resulting in a Maltese government with limited autonomy being established in 1921.

World War II Malta is the Mediterranean headquarters for the British Navy. With its submarines disrupting the Axis supply routes to Africa, the island is subjected to a long and intense aerial bombardment – one of the worst in history. By 1942, Malta is pushed to the brink of starvation and surrender. In a last-ditch effort, Operation Pedestal brings in supplies that carry Malta through its darkest hour. Malta's contribution to World War II is recognized with the George Cross – the only time the medal has been awarded to an entire nation.

1964 Malta gains independence from Britain as a constitutional monarchy.

1974 Malta becomes a Republic. All titles of nobility are abolished.

1979 The last British and NATO troops are ejected from Malta by Dom Mintoff's socialist government, and Malta formally becomes a Non-Aligned Country.

2004 Malta joins the European Union as a full member.

2008 Malta adopts the euro and becomes part of the Schengen visa (open borders) area within the EU.

2017 Malta loses one of its most famous landmarks, the Azure Window, which crumbles into the sea.

2019 Daphne Caruana Galizia, the acclaimed investigative journalist, is killed when a bomb explodes under her car.

2020 The worldwide Covid-19 pandemic hits Malta; the country controls the virus well and becomes the first in the world to vaccinate 70% of its population.

2023 Malta officially joins the UN Security Council.

2024 Five migrants die and a further eight are injured as their boat capsizes off the coast of Malta.

Language

Malti ("Maltese" in English) has its roots in the Arabic of western North Africa, but has gathered many words and influences from Italian, English, French, German and Spanish; in fact, it's a mishmash of all these languages. Though a Semitic language, Maltese is written in a Roman script that evolved at the beginning of the twentieth century: Italian was Malta's default language up to 1934, when it was officially replaced by Maltese and English. Virtually everyone speaks excellent English, and many street signs, shop names, restaurant menus and so on are in English only. Most Maltese speak a hybridized form of Maltese-English in everyday discourse, and a sizeable minority speak English only. Given this situation, the locals don't expect you to attempt to speak Maltese. It's fine (and certainly not offensive) to stick to English, and just learn the basics of Maltese pronunciation in order to get to grips with place names.

The Maltese alphabet has 29 letters – five vowels (as in English) and 24 consonants (some of which will be new): a, b, ċ, d, e, f, g, ġ, h, ħ, i, j, k, l, m, n, għ, o, p, q, r, s, t, u, v, w, x, ż, z. Pronunciation of most of the letters differs from English, in that emphasis is placed on a drawn-out twang, resulting in a sing-song rhythm of conversation. Instances of markedly unusual pronunciation are listed below.

Maltese pronunciation

ċ as **ch** in church
e as in bet
g is hard, as in **g**oat
ġ is soft, as in **j**oke
h is silent (except at the end of a word, when it's pronounced like ħ)
ħ is strong and definite, as in **h**ail
i as the English e in b**ee**
j as in **y**es
gh is silent in most instances
q is a glottal stop – the sound in the beginning and middle of "uh-oh" or the sound of the two ts in the cockney pronunciation of "bottle"
x is an English "sh", as in **sh**ear
ż is soft, as in **z**ebra
z as in ba**ts**

Glossary

aljotta traditional fish soup
awguri best wishes / happy birthday
auberge an inn of residence for a group of Knights forming a particular Langue
baħar sea
bajja bay
bieb generic name for a door or doorway; also the gate to a fortified city
bigilla a dip made of local broad beans
bonġu good morning
bonswa good evening
bragioli a traditional baked dish of steak with a mincemeat stuffing
cavalier tower within fortifications that acts a raised gun platform and rearguard position
ċaw so long, like the Italian ciao

corsair sea-based pirate licensed by the state to carry out piracy against a defined enemy
dagħjsa boat
demi-bastion a small bastion with one flank
fat ladies generic term for well-endowed stone figures and statues from the Neolithic era
festa generally refers to the three-day summer festivals held to commemorate parish saints; also public holidays
fejn where?
forn bakery
fortizza fort
garigue rugged stretches of rocky landscape with pockets of soil that support plant life
ġbejna small round cheese made from local sheep's or goat's milk

għar cave

għassa tal-pulizija police station

għolja hill

globigerina local limestone used in many Maltese buildings

ġnien garden

Grand Master the absolute ruler of the Knights of Malta

grazzi thank you (**grazzi hafna** means thank you very much)

gvern government

gżira island

ħobża bread roll or loaf of bread

ħut fish

il-belt city, usually applied to Valletta

spiżerija pharmacy

iva yes

jekk jogħġbok please

karrozza car

kastell castle

kemm how much?

knisja church

lampuka (singular **lampuki**) dolphin fish or mahi mahi, traditionally fished in early to late autumn

Langue a grouping of the Knights of Malta, defined by the region from which they originated

le no

luzzu colourful vernacular wooden fishing boats

misraħ square or clearing

mużew museum

parroċċa parish

pastizzi (singular **pastizz**) puff pastry pocket stuffed with mushy peas or ricotta

periklu danger

pjazza town square or piazza

posta post office

pulizija police

saħħa literally translates to health or good health, also used to mean good bye

San or **Sant'** (female **Santa**) saint

skużani excuse me / sorry

spnotta sea bass

sqaq alley

tabib doctor

tal-linja bus

tempju shrine, usually in reference to a Neolithic temple

torri tower

triq street or road

vapur ship

wied valley

Publishing Information
Third Edition 2024

Distribution
UK, Ireland and Europe
Apa Publications (UK) Ltd; sales@roughguides.com
United States and Canada
Ingram Publisher Services; ips@ingramcontent.com
Australia and New Zealand
Booktopia; retailer@booktopia.com.au
Worldwide
Apa Publications (UK) Ltd; sales@roughguides.com
Special Sales, Content Licensing and CoPublishing
Rough Guides can be purchased in bulk quantities at discounted prices. We can create special editions, personalised jackets and corporate imprints tailored to your needs. sales@roughguides.com.
roughguides.com

Printed in Czech Republic

This book was produced using **Typefi** automated publishing software.

A catalogue record for this book is available from the British Library
The publishers and authors have done their best to ensure the accuracy and currency of all the information in **Pocket Rough Guide Malta & Gozo**, however, they can accept no responsibility for any loss, injury, or inconvenience sustained by any traveller as a result of information or advice contained in the guide.

Rough Guide Credits

Editor: Lizzie Horrocks
Cartography: Carte
Picture editor: Piotr Kala
Picture manager: Tom Smyth
Layout: Ankur Guha
Original design: Richard Czapnik
Head of DTP and Pre-Press: Rebeka Davies
Head of Publishing: Sarah Clark

About the author

Daniel Stables is a travel writer based in Manchester, UK. He writes travel articles for *National Geographic* and the BBC, and has authored or contributed to more than thirty travel books on destinations worldwide. He also hosts a podcast, *Hungry Ghosts*, about food and travel. You can find his work on X @DanStables, Instagram @DanStabs, or his website Ⓦ danielstables.co.uk.

Help us update

We've gone to a lot of effort to ensure that this edition of the **Pocket Rough Guide Malta & Gozo** is accurate and up-to-date. However, things change – places get "discovered", opening hours are notoriously fickle, restaurants and rooms raise prices or lower standards. If you feel we've got it wrong or left something out, we'd like to know, and if you can remember the address, the price, the hours, the phone number, so much the better.

Please send your comments with the subject line "**Pocket Rough Guide Malta & Gozo Update**" to mail@uk.roughguides.com. We'll credit all contributions and send a copy of the next edition (or any other Rough Guide if you prefer) for the very best emails.

Photo Credits

(Key: T-top; C-centre; B-bottom; L-left; R-right)

Aaron Briffa/viewingmalta.com 21C, 22T, 23T
Anthea Hamilton & Nicholas Byrne/ Malta Contemporary Art 38
Brian Grech/InterContinental Malta 126/127
Caffe Cordina 18C
Chen Weizhong/viewingmalta.com 23B
Clive Vella/viewingmalta.com 99
Denise Wilkins/viewingmalta.com 119
Dragana Rankovic/Hole in the Wall 63
Fernandō Gastrotheque 62
iStock 4, 5, 11B, 12B, 14T, 15B, 18T, 19B, 24/25, 32, 40, 47, 59, 64, 65, 72, 87, 95, 101, 107, 111, 116
Janos Grapow & Daniele Cavadini/ Luna The Restaurant 79
Jonathan Xuereb/Christine X Art Gallery 60
Jürgen Scicluna/viewingmalta.com 11T, 17B, 50, 85, 115

Malcolm Debono/viewingmalta. com 10
Mario Galea/MTA 21T, 66, 136/137
Mark Cassar 45
Mithna 91
Norbert Vella/One80 93
Reuben Piscopo/Cek Cik 41
Shutterstock 1, 2TL, 2BL, 2MC, 2BC, 14B, 15T, 16T, 17T, 18B, 19C, 20B, 20C, 21B, 22C, 26, 34, 43, 53, 54, 55, 58, 68, 69, 70, 71, 73, 75, 76, 77, 78, 86, 92, 97, 102, 103, 108, 110, 112, 113, 117, 118, 120, 122, 124, 125
Sylvaine Poitau/Apa Publications 88, 121
Terronne 6
Victor Pasmore Gallery 31
viewingmalta.com 12T, 13T, 13B, 16B, 19T, 20T, 22B, 23B, 37, 81, 94
viewingmalta.com/The Malta Classic Car Museum 82

Cover: Marsaxlokk **Marcin Jucha/ Shutterstock**

Index

NOTES

NOTES